RICHARD
ALLEN

RICHARD ALLEN

❦

Steve Klots

Senior Consulting Editor
Nathan Irvin Huggins
Director
W.E.B. Du Bois Institute for Afro-American Research
Harvard University

CHELSEA HOUSE PUBLISHERS
New York   Philadelphia

Chelsea House Publishers
Editor-in-Chief Remmel Nunn
Managing Editor Karyn Gullen Browne
Copy Chief Juliann Barbato
Picture Editor Adrian G. Allen
Art Director Maria Epes
Deputy Copy Chief Mark Rifkin
Assistant Art Director Loraine Machlin
Manufacturing Manager Gerald Levine
Systems Manager Rachel Vigier
Production Manager Joseph Romano
Production Coordinator Marie Claire Cebrián

Black Americans of Achievement
Senior Editor Richard Rennert

Staff for RICHARD ALLEN
Associate Editor Ellen Scordato
Copy Editor Brian Sookram
Editorial Assistant Leigh Hope Wood
Picture Researcher Wendy P. Wills
Designer Ghila Krajzman
Cover Illustration Hrana Janto and William Giese

First Printing

1 3 5 7 9 8 6 4 2

Library of Congress Cataloging-in-Publication Data

Klots, Steve.
   Richard Allen: religious leader and social activist
/ by Steve Klots.
      p.   cm.—(Black Americans of achievement)
   Includes bibliographical references.
   Summary: Describes the life of the Afro-American leader who rose
from slavery to become a minister, founded the African Methodist
Episcopal Church, and participated in the first National Negro
Convention.
   ISBN 1-55546-570-6
      0-7910-0229-2 (pbk.)
   1. Allen, Richard, 1760–1831—Juvenile literature.   2. African
Methodist Episcopal Church—Bishops—Biography—Juvenile litera-
ture.   3. Methodist Church—United States—Bishops—Biography—
Juvenile literature.   [1. Allen, Richard., 1760–1831.   2.
Clergy.   3.Afro-Americans—Biography.]   I. Title.   II. Series.
BX8449.A6K46 1990
287'.8'092—dc20   89-49599
[B]   CIP
[92]   AC

Frontispiece: *Bethel Church
(also known as Mother Bethel) in
Philadelphia, Pennsylvania,
founded by Richard Allen in
1794.*

CONTENTS

———— ✿ ————

On Achievement   7
Coretta Scott King

1
The Protest at St. George's   11

2
The Bitter Pill of Slavery   19

3
Establishing an African Church   29

4
"To Build Each Other Up"   45

5
Independence for Bethel   57

6
A Bishop Fighting for His Church   69

7
"Steadfastness in the African Cause"   81

8
"Monuments of Glory"   97

Chronology   107

Further Reading   108

Index   109

BLACK AMERICANS OF ACHIEVEMENT

Ralph Abernathy
civil rights leader

Muhammad Ali
heavyweight champion

Richard Allen
religious leader and social activist

Louis Armstrong
musician

Arthur Ashe
tennis great

Josephine Baker
entertainer

James Baldwin
author

Benjamin Banneker
scientist and mathematician

Amiri Baraka
poet and playwright

Count Basie
bandleader and composer

Romare Bearden
artist

James Beckwourth
frontiersman

Mary McLeod Bethune
educator

Blanche Bruce
politician

Ralph Bunche
diplomat

George Washington Carver
botanist

Charles Chesnutt
author

Bill Cosby
entertainer

Paul Cuffe
merchant and abolitionist

Father Divine
religious leader

Frederick Douglass
abolitionist editor

Charles Drew
physician

W.E.B. Du Bois
scholar and activist

Paul Laurence Dunbar
poet

Katherine Dunham
dancer and choreographer

Marian Wright Edelman
civil rights leader and lawyer

Duke Ellington
bandleader and composer

Ralph Ellison
author

Julius Erving
basketball great

James Farmer
civil rights leader

Ella Fitzgerald
singer

Marcus Garvey
black-nationalist leader

Dizzy Gillespie
musician

Prince Hall
social reformer

W. C. Handy
father of the blues

William Hastie
educator and politician

Matthew Henson
explorer

Chester Himes
author

Billie Holiday
singer

John Hope
educator

Lena Horne
entertainer

Langston Hughes
poet

Zora Neale Hurston
author

Jesse Jackson
civil rights leader and politician

Jack Johnson
heavyweight champion

James Weldon Johnson
author

Scott Joplin
composer

Martin Luther King, Jr.
civil rights leader

Alain Locke
scholar and educator

Joe Louis
heavyweight champion

Ronald McNair
astronaut

Malcolm X
militant black leader

Thurgood Marshall
Supreme Court justice

Elijah Muhammad
religious leader

Jesse Owens
champion athlete

Charlie Parker
musician

Gordon Parks
photographer

Sidney Poitier
actor

Adam Clayton Powell, Jr.
political leader

Leontyne Price
opera singer

A. Philip Randolph
labor leader

Paul Robeson
singer and actor

Jackie Robinson
baseball great

Bill Russell
basketball great

John Russwurm
publisher

Sojourner Truth
antislavery activist

Harriet Tubman
antislavery activist

Nat Turner
slave revolt leader

Denmark Vesey
slave revolt leader

Madame C. J. Walker
entrepreneur

Booker T. Washington
educator

Harold Washington
politician

Walter White
civil rights leader and author

Richard Wright
author

ON ACHIEVEMENT

— ❦ —

Coretta Scott King

B EFORE YOU BEGIN this book, I hope you will ask yourself what the word excellence means to you. I think that it's a question we should all ask, and keep asking as we grow older and change. Because the truest answer to it should never change. When you think of excellence, perhaps you think of success at work; or of becoming wealthy; or meeting the right person, getting married, and having a good family life.

Those important goals are worth striving for, but there is a better way to look at excellence. As Martin Luther King, Jr., said in one of his last sermons, "I want you to be first in love. I want you to be first in moral excellence. I want you to be first in generosity. If you want to be important, wonderful. If you want to be great, wonderful. But recognize that he who is greatest among you shall be your servant."

My husband, Martin Luther King, Jr., knew that the true meaning of achievement is service. When I met him, in 1952, he was already ordained as a Baptist preacher and was working towards a doctoral degree at Boston University. I was studying at the New England Conservatory and dreamed of accomplishments in music. We married a year later, and after I graduated the following year we moved to Montgomery, Alabama. We didn't know it then, but our notions of achievement were about to undergo a dramatic change.

You may have read or heard about what happened next. What began with the boycott of a local bus line grew into a national movement, and by the time he was assassinated in 1968 my husband had fashioned a black movement powerful enough to shatter forever the practice of racial segregation. What you may not have read about is where he got his method for resisting injustice without compromising his religious beliefs.

He adopted the strategy of nonviolence from a man of a different race, who lived in a distant country, and even practiced a different religion. The man was Mahatma Gandhi, the great leader of India, who devoted his life to serving humanity in the spirit of love and nonviolence. It was in these principles that Martin discovered his method for social reform. More than anything else, those two principles were the key to his achievements.

This book is about black Americans who served society through the excellence of their achievements. It forms a part of the rich history of black men and women in America—a history of stunning accomplishments in every field of human endeavor, from literature and art to science, industry, education, diplomacy, athletics, jurisprudence, even polar exploration.

Not all of the people in this history had the same ideals, but I think you will find something that all of them have in common. Like Martin Luther King, Jr., they all decided to become "drum majors" and serve humanity. In that principle—whether it was expressed in books, inventions, or song—they found something outside themselves to use as a goal and a guide. Something that showed them a way to serve others, instead of living only for themselves.

Reading the stories of these courageous men and women not only helps us discover the principles that we will use to guide our own lives but also teaches us about our black heritage and about America itself. It is crucial for us to know the heroes and heroines of our history and to realize that the price we paid in our struggle for equality in America was dear. But we must also understand that we have gotten as far as we have partly because America's democratic system and ideals made it possible.

We are still struggling with racism and prejudice. But the great men and women in this series are a tribute to the spirit of our democratic ideals and the system in which they have flourished. And that makes their stories special and worth knowing.

RICHARD
ALLEN

THE PROTEST
AT ST. GEORGE'S

—— ◆ ——

IN FEBRUARY 1786, Richard Allen came home to Philadelphia, where he had spent the first part of his childhood. Born into slavery 26 years earlier, he had been removed from Philadelphia at the age of 7, when his family had been sold to a farmer in Delaware. Now a young Methodist preacher, Allen was returning to the city of his youth at the invitation of the white elder in the local Methodist church. As did most Methodist ministers in the late 18th century, Allen followed an itinerant vocation, traveling from town to town and station to station to preach the gospel. On this occasion, he was to preach at St. George's Methodist Episcopal Church, the mother church of American Methodism.

Allen found himself surrounded in Philadelphia by people from diverse cultures: English artisans, Quaker merchants, German farmers, and a large contingent of black residents, both slave and free—all vying for economic success or survival. It was an exciting place, a cosmopolitan city bustling with activity and full of opportunity. Only a decade earlier, the Declaration of Independence, the nation's charter

---

Allen's emergence as the first major black leader in the United States coincided with his return to his hometown of Philadelphia in February 1786. A Methodist preacher, he initially sought to establish a church that would serve the needs of the city's black community; he wound up fighting, however, for the rights of all black Americans.

St. George's Methodist Episcopal Church was the site of Allen's first preaching assignment in Philadelphia. He attended the church for almost two years before deciding to form his own parish.

of human freedom and equality, had been proclaimed in Philadelphia's streets. And just six years prior to Allen's return, the Pennsylvania legislature had approved one of the first pieces of antislavery legislation in the nation.

Philadelphia's liberal heritage had helped turn the city into a center of social activism. William Penn, a member of the Society of Friends—or Quakers, as they were popularly known—founded the City of Brotherly Love in 1681 as the capital of a colony based on the ideals of religious and social freedom. By the 1780s, the Quakers had become the first Christian denomination in the United States to require the expulsion of slave-owning members. Whereas the majority of blacks were slaves in other parts of the United States, in Philadelphia two-thirds of the blacks were free.

At St. George's, Allen began by preaching at the five o'clock Sunday morning services, an uncomfortably early time. He later commented on his first Philadelphia sermons: "I strove to preach as well as I could, but it was a great cross to me; but the Lord was with me. We had a good time, and several souls were awakened." Although most members of the congregations to which Allen preached were black (or African, as blacks were generally called in the late 1700s), his listeners also included white Methodists. All were impressed by the young preacher's skill and spiritual fervor.

After St. George's, Allen would preach three or four more times on a Sunday in other parts of Philadelphia. It was a tiring schedule, but the routine helped introduce him to all segments of the city's black Methodist population.

Allen felt that Methodism, more than any other Christian denomination, was suited for the black community. Later in his life, he was to say that "the reason the Methodist is so successful in the awakening and conversion of colored people [is] the plain doctrine and having a good discipline." In Allen's view, the plain doctrine was clear, easy to understand, and inclined to inspire the spontaneous, joyous worship and extemporaneous preaching at which he excelled and which his congregations favored. Good discipline consisted of both a rigorous, upright way of life, which he felt could only work for the betterment of blacks in general, and the church's staunch antislavery position, which Methodism's founder, the Englishman John Wesley, had vigorously advocated.

The combination proved itself appealing to black Philadelphia, and Allen quickly began to reconsider his itinerant status. He said, "I soon saw a large field open in seeking and instructing my African brethren, who had been a long forgotten people and few of them attended public worship." Allen preached wherever and whenever the opportunity presented itself. Through his work, he made friends with several of Philadelphia's black leaders, such as Absalom Jones, who was also a Methodist preacher and would remain a lifelong colleague of Allen's, even after Jones left Methodism to become an Episcopal priest.

For Philadelphia and the Methodists, Allen's preaching successes were a double-edged sword. On the one hand, he helped inspire new members to join the Methodist church every week. Yet white church leaders also had to face the reality that a sizable portion of their congregations now consisted of blacks. No longer were the pews dotted with only a few black Methodists.

For the church's leaders, the solution was obvious: racial segregation. Despite Philadelphia's reputation for liberalism, Methodism's previous hospitality toward the black community, and the New Testament charge that all are one in Christ Jesus, the black parishioners were gradually forced out of the pews to the back and the sides of the church, where they had to stand.

For Allen, the solution to the problem was equally obvious but entirely different. He desired to serve the needs of the black faithful, and this was increasingly difficult to do in a church where they were viewed as a burden and a nuisance. With the support of Jones and two other prominent black church members, William White and Dorus Ginnings, Allen approached the elder of St. George's with a plan to organize a separate black Methodist parish, where blacks could worship on their own. Allen had to take this step because the elder of St. George's had authority over all of the Methodist churches in the Philadelphia area, officially called the Philadelphia Conference.

Although the black membership of St. George's was large enough by then to form a feasible congregation, the elder wanted little to do with Allen's plan. But Allen was not discouraged, for the position of elder rotated among Methodist ministers, and each served a one-year term. Allen waited, then approached that elder's successor, only to receive an answer put into even stronger terms. Fearful of losing control over the black Methodist community, not only did this second elder (to whom Allen refers in his writings only as the Rev. Mr. W.) oppose the plan, he also rejected it with "very degrading and insulting language."

Thereafter, Allen and his colleagues attempted to work within the confines of St. George's. For a time, they contented themselves with forming the Free African Society, an officially nonsectarian, non-religious organization that nevertheless functioned much like a church in serving the black community of Philadelphia. Established as a benevolent society, it aided the members of the community in need—its widows, the sick, the unemployed—from funds accrued through regular dues. But the Free African Society was also concerned with the moral well-being of its members, requiring of them sobriety and an upright way of life. Allen and Jones were instrumental in forming the society and shaping its mission.

In the meantime, congregational growth continued at St. George's, and the church embarked upon a building campaign to accommodate the new members. Pledges of time and money for the new space came from all segments of the church, especially its black members. Through the campaign, the church was able to add seating galleries to its sanctuary.

For Allen and the other black parishioners at St. George's, a rather ordinary worship service in November 1787, their first Sunday in the renovated church, became a pivotal event in their life—and the life of all black Americans. When Jones, Allen,

The interior of St. George's Methodist Episcopal Church. Allen and his fellow black parishioners stormed out of the church in November 1787 after being told they were not allowed to sit in the newly built galleries.

"This must be a man of God," one churchgoer said of Allen, who was a remarkably passionate speaker. "I never heard such preaching before."

and White arrived that morning, the sexton ushered them to the newly built gallery. Being a little late, they hurried up the stairs to seats just above where they had formerly sat, assuming that these seats were open to all persons. As they slipped into the seats, the first hymn ended, and the elder opened the service in prayer. The congregation and its black members, according to Allen, fell to their knees for their Sabbath Day devotions.

While praying, Allen was interrupted by the sounds of a scuffle taking place at his side. Unable to ignore the commotion, he looked up to see a trustee of the church forcibly pulling Jones off his knees, ordering him away from his seat. Apparently, blacks were not even to sit in the gallery.

"Wait until the prayer is over," Jones replied, trying to preserve the sanctity of the service.

"No, you must get now, or I will call for aid and force you away," answered the trustee.

"Wait until the prayer is over, and I will get up and trouble you no more," Jones pleaded.

But the trustee would not wait. He called to another trustee who, according to Allen, then attempted to pull White from his knees. Allen said of this moment, "By this time the prayer was over, and we all went out of the church in a body, and they were no more plagued by us in the church." Storming down the gallery stairs and out into the streets, the black members of St. George's, led by Allen, Jones, and White, vowed not to return. No longer would they feel obliged to seek permission from the Methodist hierarchy at St. George's to form a parish because that church had proved first indifferent, then hostile to their presence. The time had come for a black church, a church that would serve the needs of the black community of Philadelphia. In that moment of confrontation, the African Methodist Episcopal (AME) church, although many years from becoming a functioning reality, was born.

For Allen, the church had to serve its people; otherwise, it was meaningless. It had to give them hope in the face of despair and shelter in the midst of chaos. But hope and shelter were not just theological concepts for Allen. They were concepts borne out by action, and he had perceived early on that a white-led church would not always be quick to act upon the needs of its black members.

Allen, however, was a man of action, a person driven since his earliest days to help and minister to his people. As head of the African Methodist Episcopal church, he would eventually go forth to fight for the rights of the black community in all segments of American society. ✿

2

THE BITTER PILL
OF SLAVERY

$\bullet$

Allen spent the first seven years of his life as a slave in the Chew mansion, located in the Germantown section of Philadelphia. Unlike many enslaved blacks, he performed the duties of a household servant instead of the more grueling tasks of a field hand.

I WAS BORN in the year of our Lord 1760, on February 14th, a slave to Benjamin Chew, of Philadelphia," Richard Allen wrote in his brief autobiography, *The Life, Experience and Gospel Labors of the Rt. Rev. Richard Allen.* He remained Chew's slave for 7 years, then was owned by another slaveholder until he was 20. Although both of his masters were kind, he called the yoke of slavery "a bitter pill" because as a slave he was never fully his own man.

Nevertheless, when compared with most slaves, young Richard's life was a relatively happy one. Chew was a prosperous Philadelphia lawyer who held several important political posts in Pennsylvania, including those of attorney general and chief justice of the high court of appeals. Rather than having to toil as field hands, Richard, his three siblings, and his parents performed the duties of household slaves. They worked in the kitchen, maintained the house, and assisted their mistress in raising Chew's four children from his first marriage and the couple's own first child.

But when Richard was seven years old, a downturn in the Philadelphia economy caused Chew's legal practice to suffer. Rather than face bankruptcy, he sold off his slaves, sending the entire Allen family to a farmer named Stokeley in Delaware, where Chew had formerly lived and where he still had business contacts. In a way, Richard and his family were fortunate, because they were kept intact as a family; in many instances when slaves were sold to a new owner, brother was separated from sister and husband from wife.

The change in their fortunes was a big one for the Allens. Instead of working in a genteel household in Philadelphia, they became farmhands, with all the backbreaking toil and long hours that working in the fields entailed. The situation was not entirely oppressive, however. Richard later said of his new master, "He was more like a father to his slaves than anything else. He was a tender, humane man."

The Allen family labored for Stokeley for a decade, during which time Richard gained several new brothers and sisters. But one day, slavery's bitter pill poisoned their life worse than it ever had before. For a long time, Stokeley's farm had been on the verge of bankruptcy. Finally, Stokeley was forced to sell Richard's mother and three of her children to stave off the creditors. From that day forward, Richard never again had any contact with those four members of his family.

One day shortly after the sale, Richard followed a group of field-workers into the woods near his master's home. Reports of a great meeting had been circulating among the farmhands for several days, and the curious 17 year old had decided to see for himself what everyone was talking about. In a clearing, he came upon a Methodist circuit rider, a traveling preacher proclaiming the gospel.

For Richard Allen, the meeting marked another moment of great change in his life—his spiritual awakening into Christianity. He later described this occurrence in almost mystical terms:

I was awakened and brought to see myself, poor, wretched and undone, and without the mercy of God must be lost. Shortly after, I obtained mercy through the blood of Christ, and was constrained to seek the Lord. I went rejoicing for several days and was happy in the Lord, in conversing with many old, experienced Christians. I was brought under doubts, and was tempted to believe I was deceived, and was constrained to seek the Lord afresh. I went with my head bowed down for many days. My sins were a heavy burden. I was tempted to believe there was no mercy for me. I cried to the Lord both night and day. I cried unto him who delighteth to hear the prayers of a poor sinner, and all of a sudden my dungeon shook, and, glory to God, I cried. My soul was filled. I cried, enough for me—the Saviour died.

A silhouette of Benjamin Chew, Allen's first master. According to Allen, both his owners treated him well.

The change that Allen experienced was dramatic and immediate. In that clearing, Allen came to see himself as a human being who was loved by God, a status that no slave trader or master could take from him. His newly awakened faith became the foundation upon which he began to build an existence beyond the drudgeries of human bondage.

Allen's first step was to join the Methodist society in his neighborhood. Under the leadership of a preacher named John Gray, Allen and the others met regularly in the forest. (A Delaware law forbidding religious meetings for blacks without the presence of a white necessitated this out-of-the-way locale.) In his new faith, Allen found more than just a theological concept of divine love. Gray exhorted Allen and his fellow Methodists to lead a more diligent, righteous life.

In addition, circuit riders, following the itinerant preaching vocation that Allen would one day pursue, traveled through the countryside extolling Christian virtues. The circuit riders, however, offered more than hope and consolation to their black audiences. In line with current Methodist teaching, they vigorously attacked the institution of slavery. In their understanding of the gospel, no group had the right

to systematically persecute another group, as happened in slavery, because all persons are loved equally by God, and according to the Christian Bible, "One must love thy neighbor as thyself."

In Methodism, Allen found a faith in tune with his own experiences. He liked the religion's emphasis on individual responsibility and its attacks on slavery. Originally just a revival movement within the Church of England, Methodism in the late 18th century was evolving toward an independent identity in America, one marked by attacking the status quo and bringing religion to the common people, including such men as Allen, who had often been neglected by the established denominations.

Allen experienced his first profound religious vision in 1777, when he attended a Methodist camp meeting in the Delaware countryside. Traveling Methodist preachers held these assemblies to proclaim the gospel.

At the same time that Allen converted, his older brother and sister also became Christians, and Stokeley gave them the privilege of attending worship meetings every two weeks. But trouble soon surfaced. The brothers began to hear rumors, spread by their master's neighbors, that Stokeley's indulgence would make the Allens lazy.

Richard and his brother grew worried. Not wanting to give their faith a bad name, they resolved to work even harder on their crops: The world would see that religion had made them better persons. The two brothers began to skip public preaching if they had work to do, even when Stokeley urged them to attend the worship meetings.

The principal founder of Methodism, John Wesley began to preach in the open air of England in the late 1730s, when church after church denied him the pulpit because his sermons overly excited the parishioners. Wesley then established a network of converts who spread his message to "build one another up" in God and help the poor.

The Allen brothers' diligence was repaid. After a time, Stokeley was heard boasting to his neighbors that Richard and his brother were better workers because of their faith. A good man who was convinced of the benefits of Christianity for his slaves, the master went so far as to welcome Richard's request for a circuit rider to come preach at the Stokeley farm, and soon preachers were making the farm a regular stop in their travels.

After several months of such visits, the Reverend Freeborn Garrettson stopped at the farm. A former slave owner who had become renowned for his tireless attacks on slavery, he was a powerful speaker whose words often moved slaveholders to free their slaves. He denounced slavery with such passion that he had been imprisoned several times for his verbal assaults.

On the evening of Garrettson's visit, Stokeley and his family came to hear the sermon. The preacher's text was a Bible verse (Dan. 5:27): "Thou art weighed in the balances, and art found wanting." His sermon was to change Allen's outward condition as profoundly as Allen's conversion changed his inner life. While preaching, Garrettson declared the sin of slavery so mighty that on Judgment Day the slave owner's sin would weigh heavily against him, and he would be found wanting.

The sermon stunned Stokeley. Allen wrote, "In pointing out and weighing the different characters, and among the rest weighed the slaveholders, my master believed himself to be one of that number, and after that could not be satisfied to hold slaves, believing it to be wrong." Stokeley was still deeply in debt, however, and could not simply free the portion of the Allen family who remained under his ownership. Instead, he proposed that they buy their freedom.

By working extra hours on odd jobs and at night, Allen and the others managed to save up enough

The Reverend Freeborn Garrett-son played a key role in freeing Allen from slavery. While visiting the Stokeley farm, where Allen was held in bondage, around 1780, the reverend denounced slavery as so sinful a practice that he convinced Allen's master to free all his slaves.

money to purchase their freedom. At the age of 20, Allen finally lifted the yoke of slavery from around his neck. Now free both spiritually and physically, he readied himself to go out into the world and make a living.

For a free black man in the 1780s, work options were extremely limited. For a time, Allen made ends meet by cutting cordwood. Then he labored in a brickyard. Because he did not have his basic needs for food, shelter, and clothing taken care of by others, as he did when he had been a slave, Allen took whatever work came his way. For a time during the American Revolution, he drove a salt wagon (he had little interest in the politics of the war). It was during these travels that he came across his first opportunities to preach.

Right from the start, Allen's preaching was received favorably. One listener at Radnor, Pennsylvania, declared, "This man must be a man of God, I never heard such preaching before." After the war ended, Allen took up preaching as a full-time vocation, stopping to work as a day laborer only when his money ran out.

For a black man with no formal education, the decision to become an itinerant preacher was a bold one. Freed slaves encountered racial discrimination everywhere they went. Yet Allen had seen firsthand how religious faith could transform a person for the betterment of himself and society. Moreover, he felt that he had a calling to help others share this chance to discover a new life. For Allen, preaching was an opportunity to put his faith into action.

Although not ordained to any official ministerial position, Allen traveled with several of Methodism's great evangelists and was present at the Christmas Conference of 1784, when Methodism established itself as a denomination—the Methodist Episcopal church—separate from the Church of England,

which after the Revolution was also reorganized and became the Episcopal church. After this conference, the new head of the Methodist Episcopal church, Bishop Francis Asbury, invited Allen to come with him on a preaching tour of the South. Asbury warned the black preacher that he might sometimes have to take his meals and sleep in their coach. A freed slave was still an unusual sight in the South.

Allen weighed the offer carefully. Although he knew it was a tremendous opportunity, he ultimately turned it down. It was too dangerous for him to travel in the South; he might have been forced back into slavery.

But before long, a better offer came Allen's way. In 1786, he received the invitation to preach at St. George's Methodist Episcopal Church, thus launching his Philadelphia vocation. ◀▶

America's first circuit-riding Methodist preacher (he covered more than a quarter-million miles in the United States), Francis Asbury became the nation's first bishop of the Methodist Episcopal church in 1784, when he was ordained at Lovely Lane Chapel in Baltimore, Maryland. He invited Allen later in the year to join him on a preaching tour of the South.

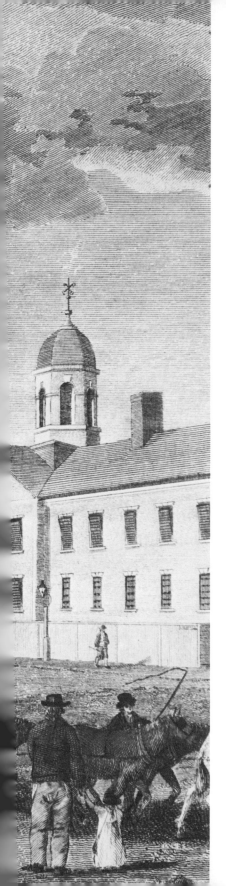

3

ESTABLISHING AN AFRICAN CHURCH

W ITHIN TWO YEARS of his return to Philadelphia, Richard Allen faced a crisis: whether or not to remain in a church where he felt unwanted. When he, along with Absalom Jones, William White, and their fellow black Methodists, decided to walk out of St. George's Methodist Episcopal Church in November 1787, they found themselves without a church. Out of that crisis the African Methodist Episcopal church was born.

Allen had little interest in joining any other denomination; he considered himself a Methodist to the core. "I feel grateful that I ever heard a Methodist preach," he said. "We are beholden to the Methodists, under God, for the light of the Gospel we enjoy; for all other denominations preached so high-flown that we were not able to comprehend their doctrine." Accordingly, he regarded his being without a Methodist church as a grave problem.

Ironically, the racial confrontation at St. George's had sprung from the Methodists' success in spreading the gospel. The church's founder and early members

Allen laid the groundwork for a black Methodist church in 1791, when he purchased a lot at the corner of Sixth and Lombard streets (now Richard Allen Avenue and Lombard Street) in Philadelphia. A short time later, he and a small group of supporters bought a blacksmith's shop from a man named Sims and had the frame building moved to the site for use as a church structure.

were vehemently opposed to slavery. But when the church membership in America grew to include slave-owning southern Methodists, church leaders softened their formerly adamant position against slavery in response to the slaveholders' complaints. By the time of the walkout at St. George's, many sermons to the black community, rather than condemning slavery, took the form of exhortations on the role of the faithful servant. As the growing church's stance against slavery weakened, Methodist congregations became racially segregated.

In addition to surmounting the trouble at St. George's, Allen faced the daunting task of establishing himself permanently in Philadelphia. He had arrived in the city less than two years earlier, and he needed to find employment that would guarantee him a regular income but still give him the freedom to serve the spiritual needs of the black community. Despite the long hours that he put into preaching, his church work rarely paid him anything more than expenses.

To establish a financial base, Allen worked for a time as a chimney sweep. He earned a decent wage clearing out soot from the chimneys of Philadelphia, because the unsavory work was essential in protecting the city's homes and businesses against disastrous fires. With his savings, Allen was able to open a shoemaker's shop on Spruce Street, where he eventually employed several apprentices and assistants.

The period after the walkout from the church was a busy one for Allen as he struggled to address both his personal needs and the spiritual and social needs of the black community. At the very least, the group that had left St. George's could count on help from the Free African Society, the organization founded by Allen and Jones to aid needy members of the black community. After the black churchgoers seceded from St. George's, members of the Free African Society began to regard the organization as a substitute for the Methodist church, and so the society took on a variety of spiritual and religious functions. Shortly after the walkout, for example, the society instituted its own marriage ceremony.

One of the biggest tasks that Allen faced after the walkout was uniting the protesting Methodists into an independent religious body. Ever since his conversion, he had been the sort of person to whom the faithful looked for answers. Allen understood that it was up to the Free African Society to serve as a substitute for St. George's, but he was appalled at the direction the organization's members seemed to be taking. In some respects, gatherings of the society had begun to take on the appearance of Quaker meetings.

The Quakers were generally well liked and respected by the black community for their kindness, honesty, and staunch antislavery position. Allen shared this respect and had agreed to a clause in the original Free African Society charter stipulating that all treasurers of the society be Quakers. Quaker wor-

A drawing of the Friends Meeting House on Cherry Street, where many of the Quakers of Philadelphia held their religious meetings. Although Allen greatly respected the Society of Friends, he preferred the spontaneous, emotional displays of a Methodist meeting over the meditative silence of a Quaker service.

ship—or meeting, as it is called—was a subdued affair, however, usually involving long periods of meditation and silence. Such worship was, in Allen's view, too different from the joyous, spontaneous style of Methodism to be to his liking. To his dismay, the marriage service that the Free African Society adopted was essentially Quaker in nature, and the society began to open its meetings with a 15-minute period of silence and meditation.

Allen found these developments hard to swallow; he had not left St. George's in order to become a Quaker in the Free African Society. Consequently, he began to avoid meetings of the group. He also met privately with some of the society's members—contrary to the organization's discipline, or set of rules—in an attempt to convince them to establish a Methodist connection for the society.

The connection never came about, however, and in 1789 Allen and the Free African Society came to

A signer of the Declaration of Independence and one of the nation's leading abolitionists, Dr. Benjamin Rush offered Allen his financial support to help build America's first independent black church. Rush also backed Allen in his work during the yellow fever epidemic that struck Philadelphia in 1793.

a mutual parting of the ways. In a meeting held on June 20 of that year, the society declared Allen "disunited" with the group "until he shall come to a sense of his conduct, and request to be admitted a member according to our discipline." The agreement left Allen free to work toward establishing a black religious community in Philadelphia along the lines he felt were best. Despite this disunion, he maintained close ties with the society and observed its activities with interest, as befitted a prominent leader in the black community.

When Allen left the Free African Society, formal leadership of the organization fell to Jones—self-educated, also a religious leader, and somewhat less strong willed than Allen. Like Allen, he, too, was a Methodist. Yet Jones was willing to follow the desires of the black community and form a tie between the Free African Society and an established denomination, even if such a connection was not with the Methodist church.

In 1791, Jones and the Free African Society drew up plans to erect a church building for the society's members, a step that Allen was quick to support. Despite his objections to Quaker tendencies in the society, Allen saw this step as a historic opportunity to establish the first independent black church. To fund the construction, he and Jones created a subscription list—a roster of pledges of financial support for the project—at the top of which were the names of Dr. Benjamin Rush and Robert Ralston, two whites who were sympathetic to the needs of the black community.

"I hope the name of Dr. Benjamin Rush and Robert Ralston will never be forgotten among us," Allen said later. "They were the first two gentlemen who espoused the cause of the oppressed, and aided us in building the house of the Lord for the poor Africans to worship in." Other prominent citizens, including Episcopalians such as Bishop William White, also lent their support and encouragement.

Their plans for an African, or black, church did not meet with unanimous approval. Officials at St. George's saw the move to build a new church as a challenge to their authority, and the Methodist elder, the Reverend John McClaskey, repeatedly threatened to formally expel the whole group from the Methodist church. One day, when McClaskey strenuously attempted to convince the group to rejoin St. George's, the conflict reached its breaking point. Maintaining that they could not remain in a church where they had been "so scandalously treated," Allen told McClaskey: "If you deny us your name [of Methodism], you cannot seal up the scriptures from us, and deny us a name in heaven. We believe heaven is for all who worship in spirit and truth." With that declaration, the drive for the first African church became irreversible.

Despite Allen's questionable status in the Free African Society, its members entrusted him with the task of finding a site for a new church. Shortly after he contracted to purchase a lot located at the corner of Sixth and Lombard streets, near the heart of the black community, the society members changed their mind; instead of following Allen's lead, they signed an agreement for a downtown lot, at the corner of Fifth and Adelphia streets, in a predominantly white section. Always a man of his word, Allen honored the contract he had signed for the Lombard Street site at great personal expense, even though the Free African Society had rejected its use. He said of the lot, "I would sooner keep it myself than to forfeit the agreement I had made."

When the day finally came to begin building the church on the downtown lot, Allen donated the use of several teams of horses for the task. According to his own account, he was given the honor of digging

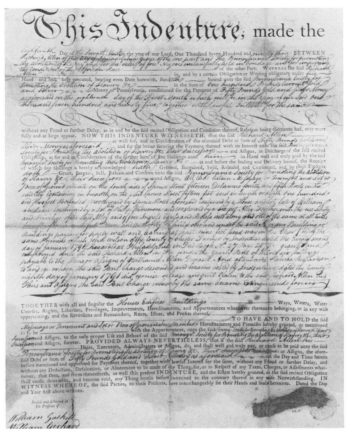

The indenture, or legal certificate, that formally transferred to Allen and the Pennsylvania Society for Promoting the Abolition of Slavery the property on which Bethel Church stood. The lot is the oldest piece of real estate in America owned continuously by blacks.

up the first spade of sod for what was to become, as he put it, "the first African Church or meetinghouse in the United States of America."

In addition to the physical labor that building a church required, a great deal of organizational work had to be undertaken. For one thing, the current elder at St. George's still refused to have anything to do with the burgeoning African church. In addition, the Free African Society had never officially affiliated itself with any denomination. The society remedied this situation in 1791, when it voted to join the Episcopal church. Although the society had Methodist roots, most of its members were unwilling to return to a church that had treated them so poorly; in contrast, Bishop White and other Episcopalians

America's first black Episcopal priest, Absalom Jones, older than Allen by 14 years, acted as the Methodist preacher's mentor. Together, they formed the Free African Society, a nonreligious organization designed to serve Philadelphia's black community, and sponsored several education projects for the area's black residents.

had supported their endeavors from the start. By Allen's account, only he and Jones voted to remain with the Methodists.

The society members invited Allen to join them as pastor in their new affiliation, but he would not renounce Methodism. Jones, on the other hand, was willing to follow the desires of the majority. Thus, when the African Episcopal Church of St. Thomas was welcomed a few years later by the Episcopal church as its newest parish, it was led by Jones, who in 1804 became America's first black Episcopal priest.

In the meantime, Allen convinced a few of his old colleagues to remain with him and form a separate black Methodist parish that, although under black control, would continue to be affiliated with the Methodist conference leadership at St. George's. Electing to make use of the lot on Sixth and Lombard streets that he still owned, Allen and his small group of supporters purchased a blacksmith's shop and had it moved to the site for use as a church structure.

While working throughout 1792 to establish his church, Allen sought recognition from St. George's as a separate Methodist church for Africans. Lacking an ordained black Methodist minister, the group had to obtain this official acknowledgment to ensure that ministers would occasionally come by the new church to preach and to administer the sacraments, which only an ordained minister can do.

The white elder again refused to have anything to do with what he saw as separatist tendencies and threatened to disown Allen as a Methodist. The question was not whether blacks should worship in separate facilities. The elder of St. George's evidently had no problem with such an occurrence, for he soon sponsored a separate chapel, called Zoar, for blacks. Rather, the issue was one of power. The elder realized that he would have minimal control over a church founded and run exclusively by blacks. It was one thing to give blacks the space in which to worship, but it was an entirely different matter to allow them to form their own ecclesiastical organization.

Allen did not want to give up being a Methodist. Yet he recognized that the black Methodists in Philadelphia needed a church in which they would feel welcome, a church that would allow them to control their own affairs and serve their community. The site of Allen's church symbolized his understanding of its mission to the black population. It stood in the middle of black Philadelphia, facilitating his intention to serve the neighboring blacks fully—in sharp contrast to the Free African Society's choice of a downtown location for the newly formed African Episcopal Church of St. Thomas.

In taking a different path to form his black religious community, Jones had given himself a somewhat easier task than Allen had. Jones had the

support of the Free African Society and his new denomination, the Episcopalians, who assisted in the
formation of St. Thomas's church. Allen attempted
to work within a denomination that wanted little to
do with him. Despite their different strategies, the
two men did not see themselves as competitors. They
both saw themselves as serving the black community,
and when the need arose, they were more than willing
to join forces.

Such a need presented itself in 1793, when the
building campaigns of the two churches were put on
hold as an epidemic of yellow fever, a disease spread
by the bite of infected mosquitoes, hit Philadelphia.
By the end of September, more than 100 people were
dying each day from the disease. The wealthier residents managed to flee the city, taking their families
and possessions with them. Most of the people in the
black community, however, lacked the resources to
leave town, and many of them died of yellow fever.

By the time the epidemic reached its height, many
of the physicians who had remained in Philadelphia
to tend to the sick and the suffering had either contracted the illness or were worn to exhaustion. Acting
out of the widely held belief that blacks were less
affected by yellow fever than whites were, Mayor
Matthew Clarkson issued a plea to Allen and Jones
for their help. "After some conversation," Allen recalled, "we found a freedom to go forth, confiding in
Him who can preserve in the midst of a burning, fiery
furnace. Sensible that it was our duty to do all the
good that we could to our suffering fellow mortals,
we set out to see where we could be useful."

On their first foray through the city, Allen and
Jones came upon a gripping scene inside a house on
Elmsley Alley: Unaware of the tragedy around them,
two children sat with their father, who was deathly
ill with yellow fever; their mother was already dead.
The two preachers made arrangements for the wom-

an's burial, attempted to treat the man, and assisted his children. After 20 similar visits that day, both men were overwhelmed by what they had seen. Each house was filled with the dead and the dying.

Under the mayor's direction, Allen and Jones systemized their efforts. Allen accepted the arduous and depressing task of organizing crews of workers to remove the dead, a job that became more and more difficult as the casualties mounted. Jones and others assisted the physicians and procured nurses to comfort the afflicted.

The first black church in the United States, the African Episcopal Church of St. Thomas was opened in 1794 and stood in downtown Philadelphia. Its congregation, led by Absalom Jones, often worked closely with Allen and other black Methodists to uplift the local black community.

In 1793, Mayor Matthew Clarkson (above) of Philadelphia called on Allen and Absalom Jones to help civic leaders combat the yellow fever epidemic that eventually claimed more than 5,000 lives. A published account of the deaths during the epidemic (opposite page) lists the number of burials from December 1792 to December 1793.

Despite everyone's best efforts, the disease ravaged the city for several more weeks; in the late 18th century, there were few medicines to treat yellow fever's symptoms and no understanding of how the disease was spread. Relief work was made all the more difficult because the stricken—victims of jaundice, fever, internal bleeding, dehydration, and despair—were often abandoned by their family members instead of being aided by them because the relatives feared the illness would strike them, too. Dr. Benjamin Rush taught Allen and Jones how to treat the fever victims with medicines and induced bleeding, which was thought to allay the symptoms of the illness.

Nevertheless, the group of volunteers could not keep up with the number of fatalities. According to Allen, it was very difficult to find anyone who would go near, let alone handle, the victims.

In the end, about 5,000 people—almost one-tenth of the city's population—died. Allen, Jones, and the members of their congregations did more than their share in keeping the number of deaths much lower than it could have been. Rush commended them publicly for the many lives they had saved. But not all Philadelphians were so thankful for or approving of the work of the black community. In one pamphlet that was published after the epidemic had passed, a man named Mathew Carey asserted that many of the black volunteers had charged exorbitant fees to remove the dead and had pilfered the belongings of many victims. It was also said that the black volunteers had displayed extreme favoritism by tending to many more black victims than whites.

Allen and Jones responded to these charges in a pamphlet called *A Narrative of the Proceedings of the Black People During the Awful Calamity in Philadelphia*, which they published in 1794. In response to the

rumors that Carey was spreading about the blacks of Philadelphia, they stated that proportionately as many blacks died from the fever as whites, contrary to popular opinion. They maintained that rather than profiting from the epidemic, as Carey asserted, the black community had given its time and money in service to the victims. The black leaders began charging for their work only when no more volunteers would step forward and they were forced to hire five men to help out. Finally, Allen and Jones asserted that Carey had been among those who had fled the city, and therefore he did not know how much care the black community had administered; he had evidently based his account on malicious rumors.

Allen's and Jones's testimony, which echoed their well-regarded reputation, was more than enough to restore their honor. Mayor Clarkson issued a public statement praising them:

> Having during the prevalence of the late malignant disorder, had almost daily opportunities of seeing the conduct of Absalom Jones and Richard Allen, and the people employed by them to bury the dead: I with cheerfulness give this testimony of my approbation of their proceedings, so far as they came under my notice. Their diligence, attention and decency of deportment, afforded me, at the time, much satisfaction.

The yellow fever epidemic in Philadelphia enabled the whole community, black and white, to see Allen for what he was: a man of his word and of honor, who found in his faith a call to serve God and humanity. He had responded to people in need by moving out of the pulpit and into their homes.

Perhaps because of his example during the crisis, tensions between Allen and St. George's eased. After the epidemic, he received official Methodist support for his new church on Lombard Street, and on July 29, 1794, a group of blacks gathered in the converted blacksmith's shop that Allen had had moved to the site. In a building where halters had once hung and horses had been shod, loud "amens" echoed in thanks for the new church. Allen's old colleague, Bishop Asbury, presided over the dedication.

The church was named Bethel, a Hebrew word meaning "the House of the Lord." The name was suggested by the Reverend John Dickins, the elder of St. George's, and taken from a biblical verse (Gen. 28:19) that reads, "He called the name of the place Bethel." Dickins himself offered the dedication prayer—that the church "might be a bethel to the gathering in of thousands of souls."

With the dedication of a humble shop as Bethel Church, a place that within decades would be known as the mother church of the African Methodist Episcopal church, Allen had at last founded a church for the black community in the Methodist style he so loved and within which he found his home. The time had come for him to broaden the mission of his church—to discover and aid the neighbor that the gospel so frequently reminded him to love.

4

"TO BUILD EACH OTHER UP"

Allen delivers a sermon in the blacksmith shop that served as the first Bethel Church. Founded in 1794, the church originally had 20 members.

AFTER ITS DEDICATION at the hands of Bishop Asbury, Bethel Church functioned as an African parish in the Philadelphia Conference of the Methodist Episcopal church. Allen's black Methodist church had finally become a reality, yet its status within the Methodist fold remained obscure. Allen, after all, had never capitulated to the demands of St. George's Methodist Episcopal Church that Bethel subject itself to all aspects of conference discipline, especially concerning the authority of St. George's elder at Bethel. The Reverend John Dickins had assisted in the church's dedication, but he was not pleased with the idea of an autonomous or semiautonomous black church in Philadelphia.

To clear up this muddy situation, Allen and the trustees of Bethel issued on November 3, 1794, what would later be called the church's Declaration of Independence: "Wherefore, as from time to time many inconveniences have arisen from white people and people of color mixing together in public assemblies, more particularly places of worship, we have thought it necessary to provide for ourselves a convenient house to assemble in, separate from the white brethren."

In calling for a separate church, the group's stated purpose was not to cause any offense to their white brethren but to lessen any discouragement the black faithful might feel toward religion on account of discrimination in the established churches and to help each other in their daily life—"to build each other up," as the Declaration described it.

To realize these goals, Allen and the trustees established several provisions for Bethel's membership that gave it a unique status as a Methodist church. Although it remained subject to Methodist policy and discipline, the church would only welcome members of African descent, and the trustees were to control all temporal affairs of the church—anything, including finances, not pertaining specifically to doctrine or worship. In concluding the statement, they declared themselves a branch of the African Methodist Episcopal church in "the name of the Holy Trinity." For the first time, the words *African Methodist Episcopal* had been used.

The church was not yet a fully independent organization. In religious affairs, at least, it was still wholly subject to the elder at St. George's because neither Allen nor any other black had been ordained a minister. In addition, the new elder at St. George's, the Reverend Ezekiel Cooper, was not about to cede property control of Bethel to Allen without a fight. Standard Methodist policy held that a congregation or parish possessed its property in trust for the conference, and the elder, as head of the conference, had final control over the property. In Allen's view and in the view of Bethel's entire congregation, the church was theirs; they had paid for it, and they were not going to sign over its control.

Allen said of this conflict, "Our warfares and troubles now began afresh." Once again, an elder threatened to disown them as Methodists, and once again Allen declared that even though the church might deny them a name, it could not deny them a seat in heaven. Cooper then tried a different tactic. He pointed out to Allen that Bethel had never been legally incorporated and therefore could not inherit any legacies left to it. To remedy the situation, he offered to draw up standard conference incorporation papers for Bethel.

Allen and the trustees agreed to Cooper's offer, and on August 23, 1796, the church was incorporated under the laws of the Commonwealth of Pennsylvania. Four of the original trustees to sign the deed were illiterate and could make only a mark next to their names. What none of them knew—even those who could read—was that aside from the church's unique African membership policy, their incorporation followed the standard Methodist discipline.

The Reverend Ezekiel Cooper, an elder at St. George's Methodist Episcopal Church, refused to let Allen's Bethel Church become an independent Methodist church. Among the tactics he employed to keep Bethel under the Methodist Episcopal church's control were making threats to disown the African Methodist Episcopal (AME) congregants as Methodists and launching a legal battle to win the property on which Bethel stood.

The AME church was one of the few places in 19th-century America where men and women were free to speak out against slavery. A number of these people, including Jarena Lee (opposite page), became preachers like Allen.

Allen said later, "Our property was then all consigned to the Conference for the present bishops, elders, ministers, etc., that belonged to the white conference, and our property was gone. Being ignorant of incorporations, we cheerfully agreed thereto."

Nevertheless, the issue of property appeared to be settled for the time being. St. George's left Allen alone, and Allen and Bethel were left with the impression that they had preserved their special autonomy. Allen shepherded his flock without disruption, and Bethel and St. George's cooperated in deceptive harmony. Indeed, the harmony was good for Bethel. In its first 2 years, the church's official membership grew from 20 to 121.

While Bethel's status was evolving toward independence, Allen was forming a plan of mission for his church. Shortly after the yellow fever epidemic, he published three tracts that foreshadowed the work to which he would devote the rest of his life: helping the poor, the downtrodden, and the oppressed.

An Address to Those Who Keep Slaves and Approve the Practice was written out of Allen's belief that his black brothers and sisters enchained in slavery were the most glaring examples of oppression. In this tract, he argued in a calm, persuasive manner against the most pernicious myths used to justify the existence of slavery—that blacks were not only content as slaves but were better off that way, for they were incapable of being anything but slaves. Allen drew upon the parallels between the ancient Israelites, who were enslaved by Pharaoh in Egypt (as chronicled in the biblical book of Exodus), and the blacks who were in bondage in America. "Consider how hateful slavery is," he implored slave owners, "in the sight of God who hath destroyed kings and princes for the oppression of the poor slaves. Pharaoh and princes, with the posterity of King Saul, were destroyed by the protector and avenger of slaves. Would you not suppose the Israelites to be utterly unfit for freedom and that it was impossible for them to obtain to any degree of excellence?" As the Israelites were debased by their bondage, so, too, were blacks diminished and dehumanized by slavery—a crime hateful to the God of love.

Allen closed his tract by beseeching slave owners to come to their senses: "If you love your children, if you love your country, if you love the God of love, clear your hands from slaves; burthen [sic] not your children or your country with them. My heart has been sorry for the bloodshed of the oppressors, as well as the oppressed; both appear guilty of each other's blood, in the sight of him who hath said, 'He that sheddeth man's blood, by man shall his blood be shed.' " Allen appeared to be referring to slave insurrections, but considering that the Civil War was just decades away, his grim words were also a warning that greater bloodshed might occur.

Allen knew that helping his brothers and sisters in slavery was not simply a matter of convincing slave owners through words that their practice was wrong. He wanted to prove that not only were blacks better off in freedom, but society as a whole also benefited. Thus, his second tract was titled *To the People of Color*. In the first half of this pamphlet, Allen addressed blacks still in slavery. Having been a slave, he spoke as one who knew well the despairs and evils of human bondage and urged his readers to have faith: "I mention experience to you, that your hearts may not sink at the discouraging prospects you may have, and that you may put your trust in God, who sees your condition, and as a merciful father pitieth his children, so doth God pity them that love him." Conversion having transformed his own life, Allen was convinced God would help those who trusted in him. With faith, said Allen, the slave would have a precious knowledge and love of God that no master could take away.

In the second half of *To the People of Color*, Allen reminded the free black community of their obligation to help their enslaved kindred. The free community had the responsibility of proving that blacks were better off in liberty—that, indeed, everyone was better off—through diligence in their work, thrift, and righteousness. Not to do so would be to sin as badly as one who owned slaves, for their poor example would contribute to the continued suffering of those in bondage.

"He who knows how bitter the cup is of which the slave hath to drink, O, how ought we to feel for those who yet remain in bondage!" Allen wrote. "Will even our friends excuse—will God pardon us—for the part we act in making strong the hands of enemies of our color?" On numerous occasions when he was preaching, Allen was known to advocate even more active and direct assistance to slaves. But in this tract, which was meant for public circulation, he focused on what the black community could legally and openly do to change public ideas and perceptions about blacks and slavery.

The third tract Allen published was *A Short Address to the Friends of Him who Hath No Helper*, in which he praised persons in the white establishment, such as Dr. Benjamin Rush and Robert Ralston, who had risked themselves on behalf of the black community. In a text added to the address, Allen reflected on the words of Jesus from the Gospel of Matthew (Matt. 25:40): "Truly, I say to you, as you did it to one of the least of these my brethren, you did it to me." In feeding the poor, nursing the sick, sheltering the homeless, and helping the downtrodden, Allen was saying, it is as if a person is doing the same for God; one is truly doing God's work.

All told, Allen was a reformer. In attacking slavery, he hoped to do more than just treat the symptoms of a national illness. He wanted to remove the illness itself, to reform the sick society. Slavery itself would have to be abolished, and for this purpose he frequently attacked the institution of slavery in his writings and sermons. But for society to change truthfully, all persons—both white and black—would themselves have to change. For Allen, this need demanded a change in the moral as well as the political fabric of the nation, a return to righteousness.

These three pieces contained Allen's vision for Bethel Church. The church's stated purpose, beyond providing a separate worship facility for the black community, was "to build each other up." With faith in a just, righteous, and loving God at the center, Allen was attempting to build a church where the black faithful could find strength and hope and through the example of their life go out into the world and do God's work. Most importantly, they would be working on behalf of their enslaved brothers and sisters. In his vision for Bethel Church, Allen saw that the church's neighbors were not just fellow Philadelphians but the poor, the enslaved, the downtrodden—all children of God who needed help.

Inspired with this vision, Bethel Church continued to grow, adding new members each year. The church soon started a school for the formal education of the black community, because Allen recognized that education was the key to real success and stability.

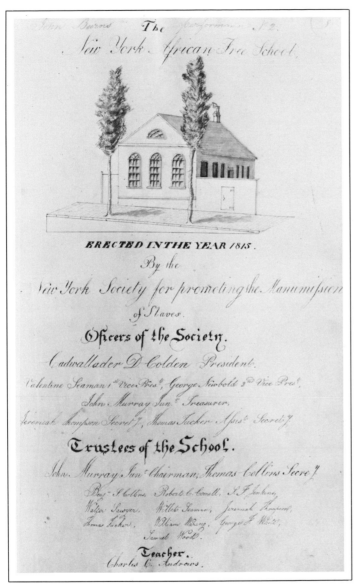

Like the Free African Society co-founded by Allen, the New York Free African School was one of several organizations formed by blacks to build themselves up as a people. The emergence of such groups gave Allen confidence that other blacks were eager to fight the same battles that he was.

Free for the time being from interference by St. George's, Allen settled into a routine at the church and his shoemaker's shop—no matter what kind or amount of work he did for Bethel, the countless hours he toiled on behalf of the church were without pay— preaching several times each Sunday at Bethel on his vision of the gospel. For a time, he focused on building up the strength of the community, that Bethel might serve as a witness to the work of God. But he did not forget his calling to serve all persons in need. When the occasion arose, he opened the doors of Bethel to anyone who needed help.

Allen did just that on July 22, 1795, when 30 slaves from Jamaica who had been freed by their master, David Barclay, arrived in Philadelphia. The Society for the Improving of the Conditions of the Free Blacks turned to Allen for help. Not only did he agree to help the freed slaves, but he and the trustees also turned the church into temporary housing for the group until such time that work and homes could be found for them.

In the early years of Bethel Church, Allen maintained friendly ties with Bishop Asbury, who came to the church about once a year to preach. Although Allen handled most of the pastoral responsibilities of the church, he was still not ordained and had to rely on St. George's for regular visitations by white clergy. This situation continued until 1799, when Asbury ordained Allen a deacon, the first step in the process of becoming a minister. Allen became the first black man ordained to the deaconate in the Methodist church. Just as significantly, Asbury took the step a year before such action was authorized by the general conference of the Methodist denomination. Asbury had enough confidence in and respect for Allen that he did not feel church approval for the step was necessary.

During this time, Allen began to hear of the efforts of blacks in other parts of the country to build themselves up. In Baltimore, a group of black Methodists had walked out of their church at about the same time as Allen and his colleagues had walked out of St. George's. Under the leadership of Daniel Coker, a former slave who had fled to New York and then arranged to purchase his freedom, the group was struggling to establish an identity for itself by organ-

izing Bethel Church, Baltimore, and a school for free
blacks. Similarly, blacks were forming organizations
resembling the Free African Society in other cities,
including New York, Boston, and Newport, Rhode
Island. Although it would be many years before such
groups would be able to join together to form a national black organization, their mere existence proved
that blacks elsewhere were fighting the same fight as
Allen.

In 1800, Allen's settled routine of work at the
shoemaker's shop and in church changed dramatically. After years of solitary toil on behalf of others,
he was introduced to a young woman named Sarah
who had grown up in southern Virginia in Isle of
Wight County. Like Allen, she had been born a
slave, and as a result little is known about her early
years. By the time the two had met, however,
Sarah—either by manumission or by flight to the
North—had gained her freedom.

Within the year, Richard Allen and Sarah were
married, and within another year their first son, Richard, Jr., was born. For the elder Allen, these changes
meant he was no longer supporting only himself. But
rather than give up his unpaid work at Bethel, he
took on additional jobs to support his family.

Although Allen's time was now split among three
pressing obligations—his work, Bethel, and his family, which would eventually include six children—
he remained motivated by one unifying theme: his
faith. For Allen, his faith guaranteed that whatever
he did—be it earning a living as a shoemaker, nur-
turing his family at home, or pastoring his flock at
Bethel—would have a purpose and a meaning.

By the age of 40, Allen had achieved a good deal.
He had started a business, a family, and a Methodist
church. The time had come, however, for the seeds
he had planted to grow for the greater good. ◆

*Allen's wife, Sarah, actively as-
sisted her husband in his work at
the AME church. According to
several prominent black clergy-
men, including Morris Brown,
William Paul Quinn, and John
Cornish, she was "a pillar [of]
the building, a mother in Israel."*

5

INDEPENDENCE
FOR BETHEL

THE PERIOD OF harmony following Bethel's incorporation was evidently good for the church. By 1804, Bethel's congregation had increased enormously, to 456 registered members, more than 22 times the original 20, and the church held several worship services each week. Allen's vision for Bethel Church as a place where the black community could build itself up was a growing reality.

But in 1805, the Reverend James Smith, the elder at St. George's that year, shattered the deceptive peace between Bethel Church and the white-controlled Philadelphia Conference. During nearly 10 years of amicable coexistence between Bethel and St. George's Methodist Episcopal Church, Allen and the trustees of Bethel had been working under the impression that they had full control of the church in all temporal matters, which included the appointment of preachers for worship services. Smith apparently felt that he should show Allen and the congregation at Bethel the true nature of Bethel's incorporation.

Bethel African Methodist Episcopal Church, as the exterior looked after the building was reconstructed in 1805. The church was subsequently rebuilt in 1841 and 1889.

The Reverend James Smith, an elder at St. George's Methodist Episcopal Church, attempted to gain control of Bethel Church in 1805 by forbidding Allen and his parishioners from holding any religious services. Allen countered Smith's actions by having his congregation pass a set of amendments, known as the African Supplement, that took control of the church away from the Philadelphia Conference, which had authority over all the Methodist churches in the area, and instead gave the governing powers to Bethel's trustees.

Allen described how the illusion was smashed, saying, "Smith soon waked us up by demanding the keys and books of the church, and forbid us holding any meetings except by orders from him." At last, it was revealed that when St. George's elder Ezekiel Cooper had drawn up Bethel's incorporation papers in 1795, he had duped the church into signing over control of its affairs to the conference. For Allen, the news was a shock.

Faced with a grim situation, Allen and Bethel's trustees sought the counsel of Joseph McKean, an attorney. McKean informed them that, as the incorporation stood, Smith and the conference could rightly demand the keys and books of the church. But Bethel was not without hope. Because the trustees of the church had approved the original incorporation, McKean concluded, they could, with the approval of two-thirds of the congregation, alter it to give control of Bethel back to Bethel Church.

Allen acted quickly and had McKean draw up a set of amendments to the original articles, which Allen presented to the congregation. "It was unanimously agreed to, by both male and female," Allen recalled. "We had another incorporation drawn that took the church from Conference, and got it passed, before the elder knew anything about it." This set of amendments, known as the African Supplement, specifically gave control of the property and preaching appointments to the trustees of Bethel. These amendments became legal on March 24, 1807.

According to Allen, the African Supplement caused "a considerable rumpus." Elder Smith was outraged that Bethel had acted without his approval and contended that the supplement would not be valid until he had signed it. Conference officials tried to convince Allen to repeal it. The supplement, after all, directly contradicted conference discipline.

Although issuing the African Supplement was a bold step, Allen had not yet made a clean break from the conference. The supplement contained the usual affirmation of conference loyalty, and Bethel depended on occasional visits from white ministers to administer the sacraments of baptism and communion. But Allen felt that Bethel's unique situation merited a relationship with the conference unlike any other church's—one that went against the norm. The elder of St. George's still had the right to preach once a week at Bethel, but if he neglected this responsibility, the trustees assumed the right to name a replacement.

Because Allen and the trustees would not repeal the supplement, Smith decided to exercise his right to the pulpit at Bethel. He demanded, however, a payment of $600 per year. At that time, $600 was a considerable amount of money, especially for a church that could not even pay its own pastor. Smith finally lowered his price to $200, to be paid directly to the treasurer of St. George's church. Although Bethel was not happy with this arrangement—the $200 seemed to be tribute money to St. George's rather than payment to the elder for his work—it was the best the church could do, and the trustees accepted the offer.

The African Supplement did not make Bethel and the African Methodist Episcopal church wholly independent, but it achieved far more than a simple undoing of the damage done by the original incorporation. It clearly stated that Bethel's position was unique, and for the first time it began to be evident that there were irreconcilable differences between the black Methodist church and the white conference.

At about this same time, Allen had another disturbing experience that may have further convinced him of the difficulty that blacks, even free blacks, faced in participating fully in white-controlled institutions. One day when Allen was at home, there was a knock on his door. Opening it, he saw before him a constable and a southern slave speculator.

Slave speculators—or slavers, as they were sometimes called—bought the rights to runaway slaves and then went north to capture and sell the runaways at a profit. Sometimes, these speculators were merely looking to get a slave for nothing, and they would accuse any likely candidate of being a runaway; the accused then had to prove that he or she was free. This slaver had singled out Allen as his quarry.

After explaining the situation to Allen, who was well known throughout Philadelphia, the constable, whose duty it was to arrest the clergyman, merely asked him, "Mr. Allen, you will soon come down to Alderman Todd's office will you?" When Allen presented himself downtown, the slaver swore that Allen was a runaway who had fled the South a few years

earlier. The case was absurd; everyone but the slaver knew that Allen had lived in Philadelphia for more than 20 years. Moreover, he was highly respected by all segments of the city's population for his work at Bethel, his efforts during the yellow fever epidemic, and countless other charitable acts.

The case was dismissed, but Allen was not happy. He said, "If it had not been for the kindness of the officer, I might have been dragged through the streets like a felon." Allen consulted with Isaac Hooper, a Quaker lawyer he knew and trusted, and on his advice Allen commenced a suit against the slaver for false accusation and perjury. When the slaver could not pay $800 in bail, he was thrown into debtor's prison. After three months, Allen dropped the suit, having taught the slaver a lesson.

On the one hand, the incident merely increased Allen's stature in the community: He had forcefully made his point and had acted with honor but had

An engraving, published in an antislavery almanac, of a freeman in the North being captured by slavers and sold into bondage. Allen faced a similar fate in the early 1800s, when a profit-hungry slave speculator showed up at the pastor's door and falsely claimed that Allen was a runaway slave.

not been overly vindictive. On the other hand, it also proved to Allen the instability of his position. At any time, all that he had worked for could be threatened; he could be taken from his growing church or from his wife and children. Similarly, his church, Bethel, was trying to build up the black community, which if anything was in an even more precarious position than Allen. Given the situation, Allen had to wonder if it were possible for Bethel and the African Methodist Episcopal church to fulfill their mission without being fully controlled by blacks.

Keeping these thoughts in mind, Allen continued his efforts to help the black community serve its members so that they might build each other up. His work at Bethel progressed, and he began advocating more active assistance to the slave population. From the pulpit, he was known to urge his congregation to shelter runaway slaves. Sarah Allen played a courageous role in this effort, often hiding runaways in the Allen household at great risk to her family.

Allen also frequently reminded the members of his congregation of their individual responsibility as believers to lead transformed lives. The faithful were not to spend their time in riotous living, for such poor examples worked to the detriment of the black community. Rather, as believers, they were to continue God's work of charity and service. Allen's fears were sadly borne out in the confessions of John Joyce and Peter Matthias, two black men who had robbed and murdered a storekeeper named Sarah Cross in March 1808. Before they were executed, each confessed and told Allen of the immorality and drunkenness that had led them to their hopeless situation and despair.

After the incident with the slave speculator, Allen was ready to defend the independence of Bethel at all costs. He soon got his chance. In 1811, St. George's reopened the issue of the African Supple-

CONFESSION

OF

PETER MATTHIAS, *alias MATHEWS*,

WHO WAS EXECUTED

ON MONDAY, THE 14th OF MARCH, 1808.

FOR THE

MURDER

OF

MRS. SARAH CROSS ;

WITH AN

ADDRESS TO THE PUBLIC,

AND

PEOPLE OF COLOUR,

TOGETHER WITH THE SUBSTANCE OF THE TRIAL, AND THE ADDRESS
OF CHIEF JUSTICE TILGHMAN, ON HIS CONDEMNATION.

PHILADELPHIA:

PRINTED AT No. 12, WALNUT-STREET,
FOR THE BENEFIT OF BETHEL CHURCH.

1808.

The title page of the Confession of Peter Matthias, an account, published in 1808 "for the benefit of Bethel Church," of the actions of the robber and murderer of a storekeeper named Sarah Cross. Matthias was among the many blacks in the Philadelphia area who asked Allen to hear their confession and offer them spiritual comfort.

ment. This time, the elder, a Virginian by the name of Stephen Roszel, refused to administer the sacraments at Bethel until the trustees repealed the supplement. Independence was far more important to Allen and Bethel than the continued presence of St. George's ministers, and when the white ministers of the Academy Union Methodist Church offered to meet their sacramental needs, Bethel's members were quick to accept.

But Roszel was just the first in a line of elders at St. George's who continued to press for Bethel's submission to conference control. After about a year of visits by Academy Union clergy, that relationship ended, both because Bethel would not pay the $150 demanded of them and because Academy clergy were threatened with expulsion from Methodism by St. George's if they continued to assist Bethel.

One associate of St. George's, a minister named John Emory, first attempted to disown Bethel publicly and then opened a conference-sponsored church for black Methodists in the vicinity of Bethel in an attempt to lure parishioners away from Allen. These ploys did not work, however. Allen and the Bethel congregation refused to give in to St. George's demands and threats.

In 1813, the Reverend Robert Roberts, the new elder of St. George's, tried a different tactic. One day, he suddenly announced to the trustees at Bethel that he intended to preach there the following Sunday. In the past, that would have been his right. But according to the African Supplement, once an elder neglected his responsibilities at Bethel, he forfeited that right, and the trustees had the responsibility of naming a replacement. Given the existing circumstances between Bethel and the conference, the trustees informed Roberts that he would not be welcome, and they invited the Reverend Jacob Tapisco to preach.

When Sunday came, Roberts still insisted upon preaching. "Having taken previous advice," Allen said later, "we had our preacher in the pulpit when he came, and the house so fixed, that he could not get more than halfway to the pulpit." The congregation moved into the aisles to block Roberts's march to the pulpit while Tapisco continued to preach. When the elder could get no farther, he pointed up at Tapisco and exclaimed, "That man has taken my appointment!"

Sheriff's sale.

By virtue of a writ of Levari Facias, to me directed,

WILL BE SOLD AT PUBLIC VENDUE,

ON THURSDAY,

The 22d inst, at 5 o'clock in the afternoon,

At the premises.

All that brick meeting house or church called Bethel church, with the lot or piece of ground thereunto belonging, situate, lying, and being, on the east side of Delaware Sixth street between Pine and Lombard streets, in the city of Philadelphia, containing in front on the said Sixth street sixty nine feet, be the same more or less; bounded southwardly by ground of Robert Green, eastwardly by ground of Silas Porter, northwardly by ground of the said Richard Allen, and westwardly by Sixth street aforesaid. Also, all that yearly rent charge of twenty Spanish milled silver dollars, payable on the tenth day of August in each and every year for ever; chargeable on, and issuing out of, all that lot or piece of ground, situate on the east side of Delaware Sixth street and north side of Lombard street, in the said city, containing in front or breadth on the said Sixth street twenty feet, and in depth eastward seventy three feet, bounded eastwardly by ground of Silas Porter, on the south by Lombard street aforesaid, on the west by the said Sixth street, and on the north by ground formerly of Richard Allen now of Robert Green. And also, all that yearly rent charge of twenty Spanish milled silver dollars, payable on the seventh day of September, in each and every year for ever: chargeable on, and issuing out of, all that lot or piece of ground, situate on the east side of Delaware Sixth street between Pine and Lombard streets, in the said city, containing in front on the said Sixth street twenty five feet, and in length or depth eastward seventy three feet, bounded on the east by ground of Silas Porter, on the south by ground of Joseph Lewis. on the west by said Sixth street, and on the north by ground belonging to the African Methodist church.

Seized and taken in execution, as the property of the African Methodist Episcopal Church, of the city of Philadelphia, in the Commonwealth of Pennsylvania, and to be sold by

Jacob Fitler, Sheriff.

Sheriff's Office June 12th 1815.

Printed by John Binns, No. 70 Chesnut-street, Philadelphia.

In 1815, an elder at St. George's Methodist Episcopal Church, the Reverend Robert Burch, made yet another attempt to gain control of Bethel Church, this time by managing to have it put up for auction. The "sheriff's sale," which took place on June 12, resulted in a bidding war won by Allen at the hefty price of $10,125.

Despite Roberts's protests, Tapisco would not yield the pulpit, and Allen was certain that Roberts would never again suffer such a public humiliation. But a more stubborn foe took his place. Roberts was followed the next year by another elder, the Reverend Robert Burch, a native of Ireland. Burch was determined to see the conflict through to its end.

The new elder had a three-pronged attack. First, he tried to buy Bethel Church. Existing documents do not make the causes clear, but for some reason Bethel was put up for auction. To regain control of the property, Allen was caught in a bidding war with someone allegedly representing the interests of the conference. Allen finally won the property at the outrageous price of $10,125. Although this was at enormous personal cost to Allen, Bethel, at least, had been preserved.

Burch, in his second attempt to control Bethel, imitated Roberts by announcing his intention to preach at Bethel. When he began to hear rumors that Bethel would treat him poorly—to the point of using deadly weapons—were he to show up, he paid a visit to Allen at home. But the pastor of Bethel, who was ill at the time, would neither confirm nor deny the rumors that Burch would be stopped.

On December 31, 1815, Burch presented himself at Bethel to preach. But he, like Roberts, was not allowed near the pulpit. The next day, he applied to Pennsylvania's supreme court for a writ of *mandamus*, a court order, to enforce his right to preach at Bethel. This was his third and final attempt to wrest control of Bethel away from the congregation. After the judges had heard the arguments of both sides, they ruled in favor of Bethel. What good would it do, the judges reasoned, to force Bethel to listen to a man they did not want to hear?

Bethel, at last, was free. In the court decision, the judges recognized what had been reality for a long time—that Bethel was a separate church run by and for the black community, with Allen at the helm. Even though it had been founded as a Methodist church, its unique character made its continued membership in the white-controlled conference impossible. No longer would any elder try to impose his will on Allen or Bethel.

When news of the court decision reached Baltimore, Daniel Coker, pastor of that city's black Bethel Church, celebrated the victory in a sermon. Just as the Israelites had been freed from bondage in Egypt, said Coker, so had Bethel Church been freed from subjugation in Philadelphia.

For Allen, the victory was a personal one. His church, Bethel Church, was now truly free to serve the black community. Its members could go out and do God's work, to bring God's people into the promised land. The seed Allen had planted for a church in a converted blacksmith's shop was growing and ready to thrive. But now he had to ask of his church, "What more can we do?" ❧

6

A BISHOP FIGHTING FOR HIS CHURCH

O N APRIL 9, 1816, at Bethel Church, Richard Allen opened the organizing conference of the African Methodist Episcopal (AME) church, nearly 20 years after he and his colleagues had stormed out of St. George's. In light of Bethel's newly recognized independence, Allen had decided that it was time for his church to join forces with similar black Methodist churches. His mission to help the black community build itself up would not be limited to Philadelphia. He, Bethel, and what would become the AME church were ready to help the slave and free black community across the nation and around the world.

Joining Allen was a delegation of six people from Baltimore, led by the Reverend Daniel Coker, who had shepherded Bethel Church, Baltimore, through its own struggles with a white-controlled conference. The trustees of Bethel Church, Philadelphia, joined them, as did the Reverend Jacob Tapisco, who had refused to yield Bethel's pulpit despite the threats of St. George's elder. Also at Bethel were delegates from churches in Wilmington, Delaware; Attleborough, Pennsylvania; and Salem, New Jersey. In all, 16 peo-

The AME church was officially born on April 9, 1816, when an organizing conference was held at Bethel Church. Allen presided over the meeting, which was attended by 16 people who resolved to "become one body under the name and style of the African Methodist Church of the United States of America."

ple were present at the humble organizational meeting of the first black Christian denomination in the
United States.

As a first matter of business, Allen was elected
chairman of the meeting, with Coker as vice-chair-
man. Assisting as secretary was Richard Allen, Jr.,
then 14 years old. With its first resolution, the African Methodist Episcopal church became a reality:
"Resolved, that the people of Philadelphia, Baltimore
and other places who may unite with them shall become one body under the name and style of the African Methodist Church of the United States of
America and that the book of Discipline of the Methodist Episcopal Church be adopted as our discipline
until further orders, except that portion relating to
Presiding Elders."

The delegates' reasons for separating themselves
from the Methodist Episcopal church were not
theological. They embraced Methodist doctrine
wholeheartedly, and they were happy to consider
themselves Methodists. But they were African Methodists, a church for the black community independent of white control. Allen said of their new
organization, "We deemed it expedient to have a
form of discipline, whereby we may guide our people
in the fear of God, in the unity of the Spirit, and in
the bonds of peace, and preserve us from that spiritual
despotism which we have so recently experienced—
remembering that we are not to lord it over God's
heritage, as greedy dogs that can never have enough."

Like the white Methodists, the group that convened at Bethel adopted the episcopal form of church
government, meaning they would be under the authority of bishops. These bishops would be ordained
from within the ranks of the presbyters, or ministers,
a point apparently disagreeable to the Reverend Peter
Spencer, a delegate from Wilmington, Delaware,
who withdrew from the conference over this issue.
Spencer went on to lead the Union American Meth-

odist church, a separate Methodist group in Wilmington.

On that first afternoon, the conference held a vote to select the church's first bishop. Although details of the election have been lost, Coker was apparently elected, and Allen was elected to a second episcopal post. Whatever the case, on April 10, the next day, Coker declined the nomination, and the group formally named Allen first bishop of the African Methodist Episcopal church. Why Coker declined is a mystery. He simply may have felt that Allen was the better man for the job.

On April 11, at the age of 56, Allen was consecrated as bishop, thereby becoming the first black bishop of any Christian denomination in the United States. Of the 5 regularly ordained ministers participating in the consecration, one was a very old friend who was there to lend his support to the black church cause: 70-year-old Absalom Jones, who had been a priest in the Episcopal church since 1804. Jones's presence guaranteed the number of presbyters needed to make the election valid by standard Methodist discipline.

With their church a reality and Allen consecrated, the organizing conference of the AME church came to a close. Each delegation returned to its home church and reported what had happened in Philadelphia. Unsurprisingly, their actions were hardly noticed outside of AME circles. After all, the church consisted of a mere handful of parishes.

Allen had his work cut out for him. He knew that the black population of Philadelphia—and of other cities—had to be organized if they were going to fight degradation and discouragement. For Allen, the AME church was the best means of organizing and building up black identity and community. Efforts for moral reform and expansion of the black church were two of the causes to which he would devote the rest of his life.

The leader of Bethel Church in Baltimore, Maryland, the Reverend Daniel Coker was elected in 1816 as the first bishop of the AME church. He declined the nomination, however, and on April 11, Allen was consecrated as bishop in Coker's stead.

A third cause—political work on behalf of the black community—was a natural outgrowth of his work as bishop of the AME church. For Allen, advocating black civil rights was an integral part of his work to help the black community uplift itself. Both moral reform (calling on the people to lead a better life) and political activism were means by which the black community could improve its well-being. For Allen, they sprang from a yearning for self-determination.

Shortly after Allen's ordination as bishop, he was launched into the political arena by a crisis in the black community that threatened its very being. This crisis was precipitated by the formation in 1816 of the American Colonization Society (ACS) and its efforts to return free blacks to Africa.

In late 1816, less than a year after a small group of blacks settled in the West African colony of Sierra Leone, the Reverend Robert Finley and others formed the American Colonization Society, an organization that sought to resettle free blacks and manumitted slaves in Africa. Many blacks in America, including Allen, regarded the society's attempt to establish a new homeland for blacks as an "outrage."

The ACS was an organization that endorsed the emigration, and even the deportation, of the free black population from the United States to Africa as a solution to the problem of race relations. The idea of African colonization by American blacks was not new; it had become a reality one year earlier, when Paul Cuffe, a black merchant from Massachusetts, transported a small group of free blacks from Boston to Sierra Leone in West Africa. These emigrants hoped to found a colony where free blacks could escape from racial discrimination and "rise to be a people."

After Cuffe's initial voyage, the idea for shipping blacks to Africa picked up support and momentum. Like Cuffe, there were those who believed resettlement in Africa offered opportunities to blacks that life in the United States denied them. But many others who supported the idea of African colonization had a far less lofty goal. They thought of emigration to Africa as a convenient way to rid the United States of its black population.

On December 21, 1816, just months after Allen's ascent to the episcopacy, the ACS was launched in a public meeting in Washington, D.C. The Reverend Robert Finley, who founded the ACS, believed that resettlement would prove to be a blessing for American blacks. Henry Clay, a slaveholding senator from Kentucky who chaired the meeting, was more typical of the kind of members the ACS would attract. At the meeting, he called the free black population a pernicious and dangerous problem that had to be overcome.

One of the original members of the American Colonization Society, U.S. senator Henry Clay (shown here addressing his fellow congressmen) maintained that colonization would "rid our country of a useless and pernicious, if not dangerous, portion of its population"—the free blacks.

Philadelphia-born James Forten became one of the nation's most influential black activists after establishing himself as an extremely successful businessman in the early 1800s. He was not only a leading opponent of the American Colonization Society but a prominent figure in the antislavery movement.

The ACS was formally organized on January 1, 1817. Among its all-white membership were several prominent politicians, including Clay, former president Thomas Jefferson, President James Madison, and Andrew Jackson, the future president from Tennessee. Jefferson succinctly stated the society's goal: "Let the ocean divide the white man from the man of color." Made up mainly of slaveholding southern landowners, the ACS directors had no intention of abolishing slavery; they proposed to eliminate the free blacks instead. The number of illustrious men among its members helped the ACS generate great fanfare in the press—and close scrutiny by the black population, both slave and free.

A few weeks later, in mid-January, Allen called a mass meeting of the black community in Philadelphia to address the issue. So frightening was the prospect of colonization gaining popular support that more than 3,000 people thronged Bethel Church. Leading the meeting with Allen was Jones; the Reverend James Gloucester, a black Presbyterian minister; and James Forten, a black sailmaker and leading member of St. Thomas's church, with whom Jones and Allen had founded the Society for the Suppression of Vice and Immorality in 1809.

For an outraged Allen, the issue was simple. He was not about to allow black emigration or colonization be dictated by white Americans. Yet he feared that if the movement gained popular support or, even worse, support in the black community, conditions in the United States might be made so difficult for free blacks that they would be forced to leave. Allen realized that the slave population would be in a state of even greater despair if there were no free blacks left to aid and encourage blacks enslaved in the South—slaves who were his black brothers and sisters and whom he felt called upon to help.

For Allen, the issue was also one of citizenship. Part of the fight against the ACS was the matter of blacks obtaining the full rights and responsibilities of citizenship—particularly the right to remain citizens in the land of their birth. All citizens, Allen felt, deserved the privileges of citizenship. Philadelphia had often called upon him to lead the black community in its civic duties, and he had always been

In January 1817, Allen, Absalom Jones, and others stated in a Philadelphia newspaper (opposite page) their opposition to the American Colonization Society, which sought to transport America's free black population to Africa as a solution to the race problem. "WHEREAS our ancestors (not of choice) were the first cultivators of the wilds of America," a portion of their anti-colonization statement read, "we their descendants feel ourselves entitled to participate in the blessings of her luxuriant soil, which their blood and sweat manured."

quick to answer the call. He had led, for instance, the fight against the yellow fever epidemic. Even more dramatically, during the War of 1812, British troops had threatened Philadelphia, and the Committee of Defense of Philadelphia had asked Allen, Jones, and Forten to organize the black contribution to the city's war effort. In response, the 3 men led a regiment of 2,500 soldiers, called the Black Legion, which stayed on guard for 2 days until the threat had passed.

Allen was not the only black alarmed by the rise of the ACS. Cuffe was soon repelled by the group's racist views and distanced himself from them before his death in late 1817. The more than 3,000 people who crowded into Bethel Church that January were also up in arms. Colonization was a threat to all they had worked for as free men and women in Philadelphia.

The assembly took comfort at the words of Allen and his colleagues. They said that they were not about to abandon their black kindred in the South or allow whites to strip them of their identity as Americans. A group of delegates to this meeting issued a statement that read in part, "Whereas our ancestors (not of choice) were the first successful cultivators of the wilds of America, we their descendants feel ourselves entitled to participate in the blessings of her soil, which their blood and sweat manured."

Ten years later, Allen put their fighting words in a letter to *Freedom's Journal*, the first newspaper in the United States owned and run by blacks: "Can we not discern the project of sending the free people of colour away from this country? Is it not for the interest of the slave-holder, to select the free people of colour out of the different states, and send them to Liberia? Will it not make their slaves uneasy to see *free men of colour enjoying liberty?* . . . This land, which we have watered with our tears and our blood, is now

PHILADELPHIA, January, 1817.

At a numerous meeting, of the People of Colour, convened at Bethel Church, to take into consideration the propriety of remonstrating against the contemplated measure, that is to exile us from the land of our nativity ; JAMES FORTEN was called to the chair, and RUSSEL PARROTT, secretary. The intent of the meeting, having been stated by the Chairman, the following Resolutions were adopted, without one dissenting voice.

WHEREAS our ancestors (not of choice) were the first cultivators of the wilds of America, we their descendants feel ourselves entitled to participate in the blessings of her luxuriant soil, which their blood and sweat manured ; and that any measure, or system of measures, having a tendency to banish us from her bosom, would not only be cruel, but in direct violation of those principles, which have been the boast of the republick.

Resolved, That we view with deep abhorrence the unmerited stigma attempted to be cast upon the reputation of the free People of Colour, by the Promoters of this measure, "that they are a dangerous and useless part of the community," when in the state of disfranchisement, in which they live, in the hour of danger they ceased to remember their wrongs, and rallied around the standard of their country.

Resolved, That we never will separate ourselves voluntarily from the slave population in this country ; they are our brethren by the ties of consanguinity, of suffering, and of wrongs; and we feel that there is more virtue in suffering privations with them, than fancied advantages for a season.

Resolved, That without arts, without science, without a proper knowledge of Government, to cast into the savage wilds of Africa, the free People of Colour, seems to us a circuitous route to return them to perpetual bondage.

Resolved, That having the strongest confidence in the justice of God, and philanthropy of the free states, we cheerfully submit our destinies to the guidance of Him who suffers not a sparrow to fall without his special Providence.

Resolved, That a committee of 11 persons be appointed to open a correspondence with the honourable *Joseph Hopkinson*, member of congress from this city, and likewise to inform him of the sentiments of this meeting, and that the following named persons constitute the committee, and that they have power to call a general meeting, when they in their judgment, deem it proper.

Reverend Absalom Jones,
Reverend Richard Allen,
James Forten,
Robert Douglas,
Francis Perkins,
Reverend John Gloucester,
Robert Gordon,
James Johnson,
Quamoney Clarkson,
John Somerset,
Randall Shepherd.

On motion—Resolved, That the house now adjourn.

JAMES FORTEN, Chairman.
RUSSELL PARROTT, Secretary.

The first newspaper in America to be owned and published by blacks, Freedom's Journal *attacked slavery and promoted racial pride while countering racist propaganda. Allen was a frequent contributor to its columns.*

our mother country; and we are well satisfied to stay where wisdom abounds and the Gospel is free." Although many of their forebears had been brought from West Africa, Allen and his colleagues were Americans, and they were prepared to fight to remain as such.

It was not a coincidence that the other three men who joined Allen in denouncing the ACS at Bethel were church leaders. The black community was organized in the churches, and the churches had experience in such a fight; the ACS, after all, had been formed out of the same impulse that had forced free blacks out of established churches. In the end, the ACS provided the black churches a united front on which to start the campaign for black rights.

Allen, Gloucester, Jones, and Forten left the mass meeting at Bethel determined to go forth and fight colonization. As much as any charitable act they could perform or sermon they could preach, this was their calling, their work for the church and God's people. For Allen, it was now a matter of organizing his church, the African Methodist Episcopal church, of which he was bishop, and of building up this church to fight for the rights of black America.

7

"STEADFASTNESS
IN THE AFRICAN CAUSE"

RICHARD ALLEN RETAINED his responsibilities as pastor of Bethel Church when he was made a bishop in 1816. Despite his new obligations to a larger flock, he still had to preach to, counsel, shepherd, and lead his church at the corner of Sixth and Lombard streets. Bethel remained his home base in the fight against the American Colonization Society, but Allen was mindful that his congregation sometimes needed to hear a message other than a highly politicized attack on the ACS. His people had to be supported not only as a community but also as individuals.

In addition to his work at Bethel, where he enjoyed a wider audience and greater responsibilities as bishop, Allen made occasional visits to other AME churches and led the annual Philadelphia and Baltimore conferences. (The Methodist church organized its congregations into regional conferences that

Richard Allen's pulpit at Bethel Church. Allen remained pastor of the church after he was ordained a bishop of the AME church.

met every year and a general church conference of representatives from all the regions that met every four years.) He also felt a responsibility to his family— to be around them and help them in their daily life. Thus, he made a concession to his new schedule and his advancing years (by this time, he was nearly 60 years old): He gradually turned over the work in his shoemaker's shop to his assistants; then his work for the church became his full-time occupation.

In turn, Allen's family helped him. According to one bishop of the AME church, Sarah Allen was known to work all night mending the worn clothes of the church's itinerant preachers so they could go out the next day and continue their preaching. Like Allen, the members of his family understood that they had a call to help the church serve the black community.

After his entry into the episcopacy, Allen concentrated on helping the AME church as well as Bethel grow. The AME church held its first annual conferences in 1817, one in Philadelphia and one in Baltimore. By the time of the Philadelphia Conference of 1818, the church showed signs of real growth. To the original five cities represented in 1816, the AME church had added more than a dozen new churches scattered throughout Pennsylvania, Maryland, and New Jersey.

But not all the news was good. On February 13, 1818, Allen's old friend Absalom Jones died. Although the two men had taken separate paths when Jones followed the Free African Society into the Episcopal church, they had remained colleagues and compatriots in the black cause. Together, they led the fight against yellow fever, sponsored several education projects for the black community, and joined forces a final time to start the fight against colonization. Symbolizing the close cooperation between the two, Jones's funeral procession, led by the Masonic lodge

to which both he and Allen belonged, began at Bethel and ended at St. Thomas's church.

In many ways, Jones had been Allen's mentor. With his old friend gone, Allen became more determined than ever to strengthen the black community across the nation, especially in the face of the movement for African colonization. It was an ongoing battle.

Ever since the ACS's inception, Allen had been troubled by the threat it posed to black Americans. On August 10, 1817, he called a second public meeting of the black residents of Philadelphia to follow up on the protest meeting held that January. Under his leadership, the group clarified its basic complaints about colonization: Like slavery, it would separate family members from each other and would place blacks in a land without the churches and other institutions that strengthened them at home. For the

The flag of the West African colony of Liberia flew for the first time in 1822, after the settlement was established by a group of black American emigrants funded by the American Colonization Society. This Liberian flag was made from the remnants of the colony's original flag.

assembled blacks, the fight against the ACS was a struggle for self-determination.

To help achieve its plans, the ACS tried to persuade black leaders to support the society's efforts. Soon after the August meeting at Bethel, the ACS sent its founder, the Reverend Robert Finley, to meet with Allen, James Forten, and several other men charged with organizing the black opposition.

Finley came away from the meeting mistakenly confident that Allen and Forten would provide little serious opposition to ACS plans. He even maintained that Allen himself would go to Africa were it not for his old age. Apparently, Finley thought that Allen and Forten respected the sincerity of the ACS's efforts.

That much was true. Allen, for one, realized that ACS leaders honestly thought they were doing the right thing. But while he respected their motivation, he did not like their plan, nor the coercive measures they took. Forten, similarly, did not like their promises of great riches that awaited blacks in Africa were they to join the ACS. He reportedly told a representative of the society that he would rather "remain James Forten, sailmaker, in Philadelphia, than enjoy the highest offices in the gifts" of the ACS.

Allen showed himself to be a staunch opponent of the ACS even when it received the support of one of his oldest colleagues, Daniel Coker. At the 1818 Baltimore Conference, a church member named James Cole brought charges against Coker. The charges were serious enough to get him expelled from the church, for reasons held in secret by the conference. A year later, around the time when the U.S. Congress awarded the ACS a monetary grant to build a settlement on Africa's west coast, to be called Liberia, Coker was readmitted to AME membership. Yet in a stunning blow to the fight against colonization, he announced his intention to go to Africa as a missionary. He had joined a band of blacks sponsored by the Maryland chapter of the ACS.

Coker was determined to leave, and Allen, try as he might, could not change his mind. Perhaps Coker felt he could escape the stigma of his temporary expulsion only by going to Liberia. When Allen realized that he could not persuade Coker to alter his plans, he remembered that the church had discussed possible overseas mission work, resigned himself to Coker's departure, and prayed for God's blessings on the mission. After several tumultuous years in Liberia, Coker eventually settled in the West African colony of Sierra Leone.

An ocean away, Allen redoubled his efforts to expand the AME church; he remained steadfast in his faith and conviction that the strength of the black community lay in its churches. In 1820, he welcomed a new conference into the church: Charleston, South Carolina. To establish the AME church in the slave-holding South had long been a dream of Allen's, and finally it appeared to be a reality. The South Carolina Conference, however, had a brief, ill-fated existence.

The AME church in Charleston was led by the Reverend Morris Brown, who had joined the Methodist church after his conversion. Unusual among southern cities, Charleston had a fairly large free black population, and this group had heard about the formation of the AME church. Brown traveled to Philadelphia to unite his church with Allen's, and Bishop Allen ordained Brown's deacon.

Upon returning to Charleston, Brown went about organizing the conference, and it soon had about 2,000 members. But in 1822, disaster struck. One of Brown's preachers, a charismatic speaker by the name of Denmark Vesey, had organized an insurrection of the slave and free black population of Charleston. Shortly before the rebellion was to begin, a household slave, anxious to protect his master's family, leaked

In 1796, nine years after Allen, Absalom Jones, and others had walked out of St. George's Methodist Episcopal Church, the black Methodist parishioners of John Street Church (right) in New York City established their own place of worship, in a renovated stable. Three years later, they began to build their own chapel; called Zion, it became the first African Methodist Episcopal Zion church more than two decades later, when the group formally withdrew from the Methodist Episcopal church.

word of the uprising. Revenge against Vesey and his coconspirators came quickly, and he and more than 30 others were hanged.

Because the AME church was an independent black church, Charleston authorities had initially viewed it with distrust. When they learned that Vesey had used church meetings to spread word of his plot, they felt their worst suspicions had been borne out, and government officials quickly suppressed the church. Brown fled to Philadelphia to save his life. Unable to return to South Carolina, he devoted himself to AME mission efforts in the Philadelphia Conference under Allen's direction.

Allen had poor luck in a few of his other efforts to expand the AME church. Perhaps his greatest disappointment was his failure to effect a merger between the AME church and the African Methodist Episcopal Zion (AMEZ) church. The origin of Zion Church, New York (the first AMEZ church), paralleled that of Bethel Church. In 1796, a group of blacks, disaffected by their treatment at the predominantly white John Street Church, renovated an old stable to be their place of worship. Under the leadership of James Varick, Zion Church was incorporated, and it eventually worked out an agreement with the white conference for a supply of ordained preachers.

As with Bethel, this relationship proved unsatisfactory after a few years, and Zion Church found itself in a position exactly like Bethel's. All it lacked was an ordained black minister. In 1819, Allen agreed to ordain one of their members, William Lambert. But when Lambert returned to New York after his ordination, instead of serving Zion he opened his own church, thereby outraging the members of Zion.

On August 11, 1820, Allen met with the people of Zion Church to discuss the possibility of a merger. After he departed from the meeting, Zion's trustees posed two questions to church members:

"Shall we return to the white people?" was the first question that was posed.

The people shouted, "No!"

"Shall we join Bishop Allen?" the trustees then asked.

On this issue Zion was divided. Some of Zion's members apparently blamed Allen for Lambert's abandonment of their church. Others felt that Allen wanted all black Methodists under his leadership for the sake of strength and power in numbers—that, in essence, Allen merely wanted another feather in his AME cap. In any case, it is certain that a strong-willed portion of Zion wanted to remain on its own, because the church opted for independence.

Varick was eventually ordained by the white Methodists, and he became the AMEZ church's first bishop in 1823. Despite their differences and their inability to bring about a merger, the AME and AMEZ churches always coordinated their efforts in the black fight against colonization.

In a similar incident in Philadelphia, Allen also lost control over another band of black Methodists. In 1820, an argument among church members caused a small group to break off from Bethel and form the Wesley AME Church. The church soon fell into debt and reached an agreement with Allen whereby the AME church took possession of Wesley and assumed its debts. While the agreement was being negotiated, however, a portion of Wesley, under the Reverend Simon Murray, had incorporated the church.

On the day Allen arrived to take control of Wesley Church, Murray attempted to block his approach to the pulpit, much as Allen had done to the Reverend Robert Roberts in 1813. By all accounts, what amounted to a riot followed, and in the ensuing trial, the state supreme court sided with Murray and the incorporated portion of Wesley. Wesley eventually became a member church in the AMEZ denomination.

Despite these setbacks in South Carolina, New York, and Philadelphia, the AME church expanded greatly under Allen's leadership. In 1820, AME missionary Henry Harden established a branch of the church in Brooklyn, New York. Within a year, he had started churches as far north as New Bedford, Massachusetts. By 1822, Allen was able to inaugurate the New York Conference of the AME church. At the conference's opening service, Allen admonished his church to seek "union among ourselves and steadfastness in the African cause."

A skillful organizer, the Reverend Morris Brown built up a congregation of free blacks in Charleston, South Carolina, in 1817 and then brought his parishioners into the AME church. When he settled in Philadelphia five years later, he began to work closely with Allen, and in 1828, he was ordained as the second bishop of the AME church.

But it was in Ohio and western Pennsylvania that Allen and the AME church found their greatest field of opportunity—and difficulty. The black Methodist presence had begun in Ohio several years earlier, when a black church had splintered off from Old Wesley Church in Cincinnati. The new church was led by white ministers and two black preachers, a Reverend Mr. King and Philip Bordie.

One day in 1823, the Methodist conference in southern Ohio held a camp revival meeting that included a communion service. For communion, all ministers and preachers were the first ones to be invited up to the altar. The two black preachers went up with their colleagues.

Waiting to receive the cup of communion, King and Bordie felt someone tapping their shoulders. One of the elders told them to wait until all the whites had received the cup. The two returned to their seat. When their turn finally came, they, and all the blacks present, refused to budge. For them, communion was supposed to symbolize, among other things, the unity and equality of all church members, and they had no wish to take part in a discriminatory communion service.

One of the blacks present that day had been to Bethel Church, and he knew of Richard Allen and the AME church. When the Reverend George Goler,

An AME church meeting in Cincinnati, Ohio, where the black Methodist presence made itself felt in the early 1820s. By the end of the decade, however, newly imposed legal restrictions forced many of the state's black residents to move out of Ohio, thereby reducing the AME church's influence in the region.

an AME missionary, came to the area, the black Methodists asked to be united with the AME church, and the AME presence in Ohio began. The AME church did not grow quickly there, however. Ohio at the time was still, for the most part, frontier territory. Itinerant AME preachers had to cope with anything from bandits to blizzards to unfriendly white residents.

During the early 1820s, the AME church saw tremendous growth under the leadership of Allen. In 1823, he even received an invitation from the president of the black-governed Republic of Haiti to send them missionaries; the following year, a band of AME church members under the Reverend Scipio Beanes journeyed there. But while Allen was organizing and strengthening his church, the American Colonization Society was furthering its plans to return all blacks to Africa.

While Allen's successes and failures in expanding the AME church remained obscure to most white people in the United States, the work of the ACS continued to receive great attention in the press— and, ominously, in churches and law-making bodies as well. Within the first 10 years of the ACS's existence, the national conventions of the Presbyterian, Dutch Reformed, Baptist, and Methodist churches had all given the society their official support, as had some regional bodies of other denominations. State legislatures from areas as far south as Tennessee and Virginia and as far north as Vermont and Massachusetts gave it their formal approval. After former president James Monroe spoke approvingly of it, the ACS named Liberia's capital city, Monrovia, after him.

To have any effect in the fight against colonization, the black community needed a mouthpiece for making its views known to the world, and it found the proper vehicle in churches from Ohio to Maryland, which rang out with attacks against the ACS. The churches emerged as the most potent force in the fight for black rights because of the church members' unshakable faith. The AME church, with Allen at the helm, was the backbone of this network of opposition. Churches such as James Gloucester's African Presbyterian and Forten's St. Thomas Episcopal also lent vital support.

As Allen approached his late sixties, he felt the need to share some of the duties of leadership so that the church's message would continue to ring out loud and clear for years to come. In 1824, the third general conference of the AME church elected Morris Brown, the fugitive from South Carolina, to be assistant

bishop, at Allen's request. Allen was glad to have the help of a man who had experienced firsthand the oppression of being black in the South. Brown's election guaranteed that the AME church would continue to speak for those who could not speak for themselves—slaves in the South and disorganized blacks in the North.

In 1827, the black effort gained another powerful voice to speak for the cause. On March 16, Samuel E. Cornish, a former student of James Gloucester's, and John Russwurm, one of America's first black college graduates, launched the nation's first black newspaper, *Freedom's Journal*. Recognizing from the start the newspaper's potential for reaching a national audience, Allen became a frequent contributor to its columns, fervently promoting the abolition of slavery and boldly attacking colonization, which he denounced as an "outrage."

The Reverend Samuel E. Cornish (left) and John Russwurm (right) were among the black activists who founded Freedom's Journal, *a newspaper established in March 1827 "to plead our cause. Too long have others spoken for us." A staunch opponent of the American Colonization Society, Russwurm shocked his newspaper's readers by announcing in 1829 that any discussion of winning equality for blacks in America was a "waste of words."*

In the face of Allen's efforts, the ACS kept trying to lure the black community into accepting colonization and emigrating to Liberia. Very few people listened to them, however. By 1830, fewer than 2,000 people had sailed to Africa. American blacks were heeding Allen's call for steadfastness.

But the battle against colonization in the late 1820s was not easily won. In 1829, several crises shook the unity that had kept the AME church and the fight against colonization strong. First, John Russwurm, editor of the very paper founded to fight colonization—*Freedom's Journal*—announced in its pages his conversion to the ACS cause. Many considered his change of heart a betrayal, a defection to the enemy.

The ACS, to be sure, had offered Russwurm a leadership position in Liberia. Yet he had spoken favorably of colonization in his graduation speech from Bowdoin College a few years earlier, so he certainly had always been open to the idea. His switch, in any case, was a blow to Allen and a triumph for the ACS. *Freedom's Journal*, noted for its attacks on the society, ceased publication within a year.

Second, as state legislatures endorsed colonization, they also began to make life more difficult for free blacks. They could limit, for instance, the black population's mobility or tax black citizens unduly. Such restrictions were meant to force the black population to emigrate. The situation had gotten so bad in Maryland in 1826 that some members of Baltimore's Bethel Church had considered moving to Liberia, and only Allen's exhortations had convinced them to stay.

In 1829, Allen's own Pennsylvania legislature had begun to debate taking the vote away from the state's free black citizens—shortly after it had endorsed the ACS. This endorsement and the subsequent debate represented another threat to Allen's, and the whole black community's, rights of citizenship.

Allen's final crisis was the plight of the black residents of Ohio, many of whom were AME church members. Because it was a border state between the North and the South, Ohio had a fairly large free black population. In 1827, state authorities had decided to invoke and enforce a rarely used Black Code, legislated years earlier, to impose restrictions on the state's blacks.

This Black Code required each free black resident to deposit a $500 bond with the state to guarantee his or her good behavior. At that time, most whites, let alone free blacks, could not afford this bond. During the next two years, nearly all the black residents of Ohio were forced to leave their homes. By 1829, most of them had settled in Canada.

Such a turn of events had important ramifications for Allen. The drive for black rights had been shaken by Russwurm's defection, and the ACS was crowing over its triumph. The strong AME presence in Ohio disintegrated under the persecution. Similarly, his own rights as a citizen of Pennsylvania were under assault by the state legislature.

For Allen, the time had come for more immediate action. The time had come for all blacks to join together in the fight for their rights. ❧

8

"MONUMENTS OF GLORY"

Primarily a man of the cloth, Allen viewed the church as a means to uplift the black community and help his race gain its freedom. The church, he believed, could best serve God by serving His people.

IN APRIL 1830, Richard Allen received a letter from a young black man named Hezekiah Grice of Baltimore. An escaped slave, Grice had experienced the oppression of black Americans in both slavery and freedom. After he met William Lloyd Garrison, the nation's leading white spokesman for the abolition of slavery, Grice was fired up to do something about his people's plight. In his letter, he asked Allen about the feasibility of a national convention for black Americans.

Allen wrote back to Grice and invited him to Philadelphia to discuss the issue. By the time Grice arrived in Philadelphia, word had spread that a group of New Yorkers were also considering the possibility of such a convention. Allen commented to Grice, "My dear child, we must take some action immediately or else these New Yorkers will get ahead of us."

That night, a committee of five persons, chaired by Allen, began to make plans for the first national convention of black Americans. An invitation went out for all interested black leaders to convene at Bethel Church on September 15, 1830. Allen spread word of the convention through his churches while Grice traveled outside the city to bring the news to others.

When Grice arrived back in Philadelphia, he found almost no one in the city who knew about the convention. One person even exclaimed to Grice, "Who ever heard of colored people holding a convention—a convention, indeed!"

Fearful of having the convention disrupted, Allen had kept it a secret from the public. But the word had gotten out to black leaders, and before long, delegates from around the nation began to trickle into Bethel. In all, 40 persons representing 7 states convened at the church. The number of attendees was so small because many states had begun to enforce travel restrictions on free blacks.

The convention of 1830 was mainly an effort by Allen and other blacks to organize a national network of black support and cooperation, enabling them to advocate the black cause and fight the American Colonization Society. As an initial measure, Allen was elected president of the new association, which was called in full the American Society of Free Persons of Colour, for Improving their Condition in the United States; for Purchasing Lands; and for the Establishment of a Settlement in Upper Canada.

The name reflected the organization's motivations. Fearing that more people would be forced out of their homes, as the black residents of Ohio had been, the members of the American Society of Free Persons of Colour wished to explore the conditions for black settlement in Canada and to support their kindred who had been forced to move there. United in their opposition to colonization, they also wanted to fight for improved conditions for free blacks and against the coercive restrictions engendered by white enthusiasm for the ACS.

Ultimately, the American Society of Free Persons of Colour was taking aim at slavery itself. As a symbolic measure, the convention advocated making the Fourth of July a day of fasting and prayer for black

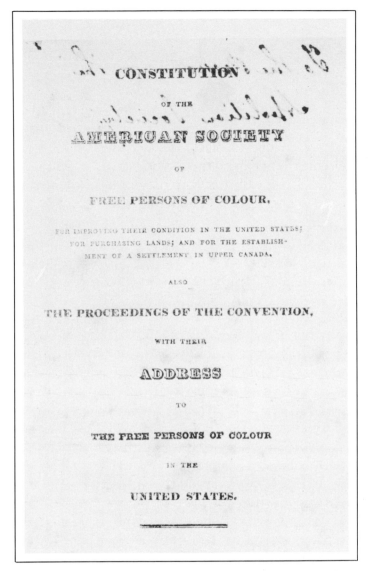

CONSTITUTION

OF THE

AMERICAN SOCIETY

OF

FREE PERSONS OF COLOUR,

FOR IMPROVING THEIR CONDITION IN THE UNITED STATES;
FOR PURCHASING LANDS; AND FOR THE ESTABLISH-
MENT OF A SETTLEMENT IN UPPER CANADA.

ALSO

THE PROCEEDINGS OF THE CONVENTION,

WITH THEIR

ADDRESS

TO

THE FREE PERSONS OF COLOUR

IN THE

UNITED STATES.

On the night of September 15, 1830, Bethel Church hosted the first national convention of black Americans. The meeting resulted in the formation of the American Society of Free Persons of Colour, an organization that sought to improve conditions for blacks in the United States; Allen was elected president of the society.

people. Citing the Declaration of Independence, they affirmed that the nation's guiding principle—"that all men are born free and equal and consequently are endowed with inalienable rights, among which are the enjoyment of life, liberty and pursuit of happiness"—was a dream as yet unrealized.

Its officers elected and its structure in place, the society ended its convention with plans to meet again

A major figure in the fight against slavery, William Lloyd Garrison edited the abolitionist newspapers The Liberator *and* The Genius of Universal Emancipation *(opposite page). "Genuine Abolition is an essential part of Christianity," he maintained, "and aside from it there can be no humanity."*

in 1831. Motivated by the success of the convention, Allen pushed for more political and economic organization. In December 1830, he organized the Free Produce Society in a meeting at Bethel Church. Members of this organization and its affiliate, the Free Cotton Society, pledged to buy only goods made and raised by nonslaveholders, when possible. Benjamin Lundy, editor—along with Garrison—of *The Genius of Universal Emancipation*, an abolitionist newspaper, had long advocated this idea, and Allen saw that it could provide more than a symbolic blow to the slave economy.

Allen did not lead the next convention of the American Society of Free Persons of Colour, nor did

he see the effects of the Free Produce Society's boycott of slave products. For several years he had been slowing down, turning more and more of his AME church responsibilities over to Bishop Morris Brown. Still, he had continued to expand his work through his strong presence at the first convention.

Finally, though, the strain of his constant efforts and the progress of the years took their toll on Allen. In early 1831, he fell sick, and on March 26, 1831, he died at home. He was 71 years of age.

Thirty years before the start of the Civil War, the black people of the United States had lost an eloquent spokesman and advocate, and the African Methodist Episcopal church had lost its founder and leader. Yet

Richard Allen left behind a legacy in the struggle for justice that would continue to grow until it blossomed into freedom.

When word reached Boston that Allen had died, Garrison extolled him and his lifelong work in *The Genius of Universal Emancipation*: "In the death of Richard Allen, the first Bishop of the African Methodist Episcopal Church, religion has lost one of its brightest, most talented, and distinguished ornaments; philanthropy one of her finest and most practical supporters; and the great cause of African Emancipation one of the purest friends and patriots that ever exerted his energies in favor of civil and religious liberty." When he and his people had been "dragged from the altar of his God," it was Allen, said Garrison, who stepped forth to lead his people to religious freedom. Garrison said of Allen's accomplishments, "His noble deeds will remain cherished in the memory of mankind as imperishable monuments of eternal glory." Such lavish praise from Garrison, perhaps the best-known spokesman for the abolition of slavery, bears witness to the magnitude of Allen's accomplishments.

Even more stirring was the testimony of David Walker, a former slave who had become a radical abolitionist. In his widely read *Appeal to the Coloured Citizens of the World*, an electrifying attack on slavery published in 1829, Walker could not contain his admiration for Allen: "It is impossible my brethren for me to say much in this work respecting that man of God. When the Lord shall raise up coloured historians in succeeding generations, to present the crimes of this nation, to the then gazing world, the Holy Ghost will make them do justice to the name of Bishop Allen, of Philadelphia. Suffice it for me to say, that the name of this very man (Richard Allen) though now in obscurity and degradation, will notwithstanding, stand on the pages of history among

This building, the fourth—and current—Mother Bethel Church, opened its doors for the first time in 1890. Located at Richard Allen Avenue and Lombard Street in Philadelphia, it was designated a national shrine in 1965.

the greatest divines who have lived since the apostolic age. . . . I do hereby openly affirm it to the world, that he has done more in a spiritual sense for his ignorant and wretched brethren than any other man of colour has, since the world began."

To look at Allen's legacy is to see that such praise is justified. At a time when a free black had barely more rights than a slave, Allen organized his people so they might take comfort and find strength in each other, their faith, and their church. He was the first black to be ordained in the Methodist church, the first black to become bishop in any denomination in the United States, and the founder of the first black Christian denomination—the African Methodist

The AME church is now the oldest black-established organization in the United States, thanks largely to the efforts of the church's first bishops: Richard Allen, Morris Brown, Edward Waters, William Paul Quinn, Willis Nazrey, Daniel A. Payne, Alexander W. Wayman, Jabez P. Campbell, James A. Shorter, Thomas M. D. Ward, and John M. Brown.

Episcopal church, now a church with branches around the world.

As a symbol of this legacy stands Bethel Church. Built on property Allen bought with his own money, it was saved from disaster when Allen came to its rescue at auction. Yet in all his years of service, Bethel apparently paid him a total of $80. The church still stands today, the mother church of African Methodism and a memorial to Allen's dedication to the cause of the black church.

Allen's family, to whom he devoted himself as well, continued his efforts. Sarah Allen outlived her husband by almost 20 years, which were spent in service to her family and her church. Their six children were also very active in the black community.

Perhaps Allen's greatest legacy, however, was the struggle for justice he started at Bethel and saw through to his death—a struggle against oppression of any kind, a fight to encourage and strengthen his people. Allen insisted on full civil rights for all citizens—black and white—and through his faith he recognized the downtrodden, the oppressed, and especially the enslaved as the people he was called on to help.

Allen did not live to see the victory in his fight against slavery and colonization. But the national convention movement, which organized the American Society of Free Persons of Colour, was part of the beginning of the end of the systemic injustice of slavery. After Allen's death, the American Society of Free Persons of Colour and the national convention movement grew into a national effort uniting whites and blacks for the abolition of slavery.

Through Allen's efforts, the American Colonization Society failed to gain the popularity it sought in the black community, and became instead a focal point for black unity. William Lloyd Garrison sounded the death knell of the ACS when he attacked it on the front page of the premier issue of the anti-slavery newspaper *The Liberator* in 1831 and in his pamphlet *Thoughts on African Colonization*, published in 1832. But it was men such as Allen, through their words and example, who convinced Garrison of the injustice of colonization.

Above all, Allen's legacy was one of hope. Through his work and his faith, he was able to bring hope into the lives of thousands of black men and women, to help them understand that their life had meaning despite the degrading conditions they had to endure. With this hope, the black men and women Allen touched came to realize that they had a cause worth fighting for: freedom and justice for all.

*An emblem of the African Meth-
odist Episcopal church*

CHRONOLOGY

1760   Richard Allen is born into slavery on February 14 in Philadelphia, Pennsylvania

1767   Sold to a farmer in Delaware

1777   Experiences a religious conversion and joins the Methodist church

1786   Purchases his freedom after an itinerant Methodist preacher convinces Allen's master of the evils of slavery; returns to Philadelphia

1787   Along with Absalom Jones and others, storms out of St. George's Methodist Church in protest of the church's discriminatory seating policy

1793   Allen and Jones organize the black community to fight against yellow fever

1794   Allen founds Bethel Church

1799   Francis Asbury, a Methodist bishop, ordains Allen as a deacon

1800   Richard and Sarah Allen are married

1807   Bethel Church passes the African Supplement, which effectively separates it from the Methodist church

1812   Allen and Jones organize the Black Legion to defend Philadelphia in the War of 1812

1816   The Pennsylvania Supreme Court declares Bethel Church independent, and the African Methodist Episcopal (AME) church is formed in Philadelphia; Allen is elected its first bishop

1817   First protest meeting against the American Colonization Society is held at Bethel Church

1830   Allen organizes first national black convention, the American Society of Free Persons of Colour

1831   Dies in Philadelphia on March 26

FURTHER READING

Allen, Richard. *The Life Experience and Gospel Labors of the Rt. Rev. Richard Allen.* 2nd ed. Nashville: Abingdon, 1960. [Contains "An Address to Those Who Keep Slaves and Approve the Practice," "A Narrative of the Proceedings of the Colored People During the Awful Calamity in Philadelphia in the year 1793; and a Refutation of Censures Thrown upon in some Publications," and "To the People of Color."]

Frazier, Edward Franklin. *The Negro Church in America.* New York: Schocken Books, 1974.

George, Carol V. R. *Segregated Sabbaths: Richard Allen and the Emergence of the Independent Black Churches, 1760–1840.* New York: Oxford University Press, 1973.

Payne, Daniel A. *History of the African Methodist Episcopal Church.* New York: Arno Press, 1969.

Walker, David. *An Appeal, in Four Articles, Together with a Preamble, to the Coloured Citizens of the World.* New York: Hill and Wang, 1965.

Wesley, Charles H. *Richard Allen: Apostle of Freedom.* Washington: Associated Publishers, 1969. [Contains "Letter of Bishop Richard Allen to *Freedom's Journal*, November 2, 1827, on African Colonization."]

Wright, R. R., Jr. *The Bishops of the African Methodist Episcopal Church.* Nashville: A.M.E. Sunday School Union, 1963.

INDEX

Academy Union Methodist Church, 63, 64
Address to Those Who Keep Slaves and Approve the Practice, An, 49
Africa, 72–79, 83, 84, 92, 94
African Methodist Episcopal (AME) church, 17, 29, 43, 46, 60, 62, 69–79, 81–95, 103
African Presbyterian Church, 92
African Supplement, 59, 60, 62, 64
Allen, Richard
  and AME church, 69–79, 81–95
  becomes a preacher, 26
  and Bethel Church, 33–37, 42–43, 45–55, 57–67
  childhood, 11, 19
  death, 101
  employment, 26, 30, 53, 82
  family, 20, 23, 55, 62, 70, 82, 104
  final years, 97–105
  freed from slavery, 25–26
  made deacon, 54
  marriage, 55
  Methodism, introduction to, 20–27
  named bishop, 71
  opens a shoemaker's shop, 30
  opposition to ACS, 72–79, 83–85
  protest at St. George's, 15–17, 29–31
  publishes tracts, 49–52
  purchases land for a church, 34
  as a slave, 19–25
  threatened by slave speculator, 60–61
  and yellow fever epidemic, 38–42

Allen, Richard, Jr. (son), 55, 70
Allen, Sarah (wife), 55, 62, 82, 104
American Colonization Society (ACS), 72–79, 81, 83–85, 92, 94, 95, 98, 101
American Methodist Episcopal Zion (AMEZ) church, 87, 88
American Revolution, 26
American Society of Free Persons of Colour, 98, 100
Appeal to the Coloured Citizens of the World (Walker), 102
Asbury, Francis, 27, 42, 45, 54
Attleborough, Pennsylvania, 69

Baltimore, Maryland, 54, 55, 67, 69, 70, 82
Baltimore Conference, 84
Barclay, David, 54
Beanes, Scipio, 92
Bethel Church, Baltimore, 55, 69, 94
Bethel Church, 42–43, 45–55, 57–67, 69, 70, 76, 78, 79, 81, 87, 88, 90, 97, 98, 100, 104
Black Code, 95
Bordie, Philip, 89–90
Boston, Massachusetts, 55, 73, 102
Bowdoin College, 94
Brooklyn, New York, 88
Brown, Morris, 85, 86, 92, 93, 101
Burch, Robert, 66

Canada, 95, 98
Carey, Matthew, 40–41
Charleston, South Carolina, 85, 86
Chew, Benjamin, 19–20

Christmas Conference of 1784, 26
Church of England, 27
Cincinnati, Ohio, 89
Civil War, 50, 101
Clarkson, Matthew, 38, 42
Clay, Henry, 74, 75
Coker, Daniel, 54, 67, 69, 70, 71, 84, 85
Cole, James, 84
Committee of Defense of Philadelphia, 77
Congress, U.S., 84
Cooper, Ezekiel, 46–47, 58
Cornish, Samuel E., 93
Cross, Sarah, 62
Cuffe, Paul, 73

Declaration of Independence, 12, 99
Delaware, 11, 20, 21
Dickins, John, 42, 45
Dutch Reformed church, 92

Emory, John, 64

Finley, Robert, 74, 84
Forten, James, 76, 77, 79, 84, 92
Free African Society, 15, 30, 31–37, 55, 82
Free Cotton Society, 100
Freedom's Journal, 77, 93, 94
Free Produce Society, 100, 101

Garrettson, Freeborn, 25
Garrison, William Lloyd, 97, 100, 102
Genius of Universal Emancipation, The (Garrison and Lundy), 100, 102
Ginnings, Dorus, 14
Gloucester, James, 76, 79, 92, 93
Goler, George, 90

Gray, John, 21
Grice, Hezekiah, 97–98

Haiti, 91
Harden, Henry, 88
Hooper, Isaac, 61

Jackson, Andrew, 75
Jamaica, 54
Jefferson, Thomas, 75
John Street Church, 87
Jones, Absalom, 14, 15, 16–17, 29, 30, 33, 36, 37–42, 71, 76, 77, 82
Joyce, John, 62

Kentucky, 74

Lambert, William, 87
Liberia, 84, 85, 94
Life, Experiences and Gospel Labors of the Right Reverend Richard Allen, The, 19
Lundy, Benjamin, 100

McClaskey, John, 34
McKean, Joseph, 58–60
Madison, James, 75
Maryland, 82, 85, 94
Massachusetts, 92
Matthias, Peter, 62
Methodism, 11, 13–17, 21, 22, 26, 32, 64
Methodist Episcopal church, 26–27, 45
Monroe, James, 92
Monrovia, Liberia, 92
Murray, Simon, 88

Narrative of the Proceedings of the Black People During the Awful Calamity in Philadelphia, 40

New Bedford, Massachusetts, 88
New Jersey, 82
Newport, Rhode Island, 55
New York, 54, 55, 87
New York Conference of the American Methodist Church, 88

Ohio, 89, 91, 95, 98
Old Wesley Church, 89

Penn, William, 12
Pennsylvania, 47, 66, 82, 83, 89, 94, 95
Philadelphia, Pennsylvania, 11–17, 19, 29, 30, 33, 37, 38, 40, 41, 42, 45, 54, 60, 61, 67, 69, 70, 71, 76, 77, 82, 84, 86, 88, 97
Philadelphia Conference of the Methodist Episcopal church, 15, 45, 48, 57, 82, 86
Presbyterian church, 92

Quakers, 12, 31–33

Radnor, Pennsylvania, 26
Ralston, Robert, 33, 51
Roberts, Robert, 64, 66, 88
Roszel, Stephen, 63, 64
Rush, Benjamin, 33, 40, 51
Russwurm, John, 93, 94, 95

St. George's Methodist Episcopal Church, 11, 13, 14, 15, 17, 27, 29–32, 34, 35, 36, 37, 42, 45, 46, 48, 53, 54, 57, 58, 59, 60, 63, 64, 68, 69
St. Thomas African Episcopal Church, 36, 37, 83, 92
Salem, New Jersey, 69
Short Address to the Friends of Him who Hath No Helper, A, 51
Sierra Leone, West Africa, 73, 85
Slavery, 12–13, 21, 29–30, 49–52, 60, 62
Smith, James, 57, 58
Society for the Improving of the Conditions of the Free Blacks, 54
Society for the Suppression of Vice and Immorality, 76
Society of Friends. See Quakers
South Carolina Conference, 85
Spencer, Peter, 70

Tapisco, Jacob, 64, 66, 69
Tennessee, 75, 92
To the People of Color, 50–51

Union American Methodist church, 70

Varick, James, 87, 88
Vermont, 92
Vesey, Denmark, 85, 86
Virginia, 92

Walker, David, 102
War of 1812, 77
Washington, D.C., 74
Wesley, John, 13, 46
Wesley American Methodist Episcopal Church, 88
West Africa, 78
White, William, 14, 16–17, 29, 34, 35
Wilmington, Delaware, 69, 70, 71

Yellow fever epidemic of 1793, 38–43

Zion Church, 87, 88
Zoar, 37

PICTURE CREDITS

———— ✿ ————

STEVE KLOTS, a native of Tennessee, holds a bachelor of arts degree from Trinity College in Connecticut and a master of divinity degree from Harvard University. He is currently studying the role of the church in a multicultural context, on a postgraduate fellowship at the University of Otago in Dunedin, New Zealand.

NATHAN IRVIN HUGGINS is W.E.B. Du Bois Professor of History and Director of the W.E.B. Du Bois Institute for Afro-American Research at Harvard University. He previously taught at Columbia University. Professor Huggins is the author of numerous books, including *Black Odyssey: The Afro-American Ordeal in Slavery*, *The Harlem Renaissance*, and *Slave and Citizen: The Life of Frederick Douglass*.